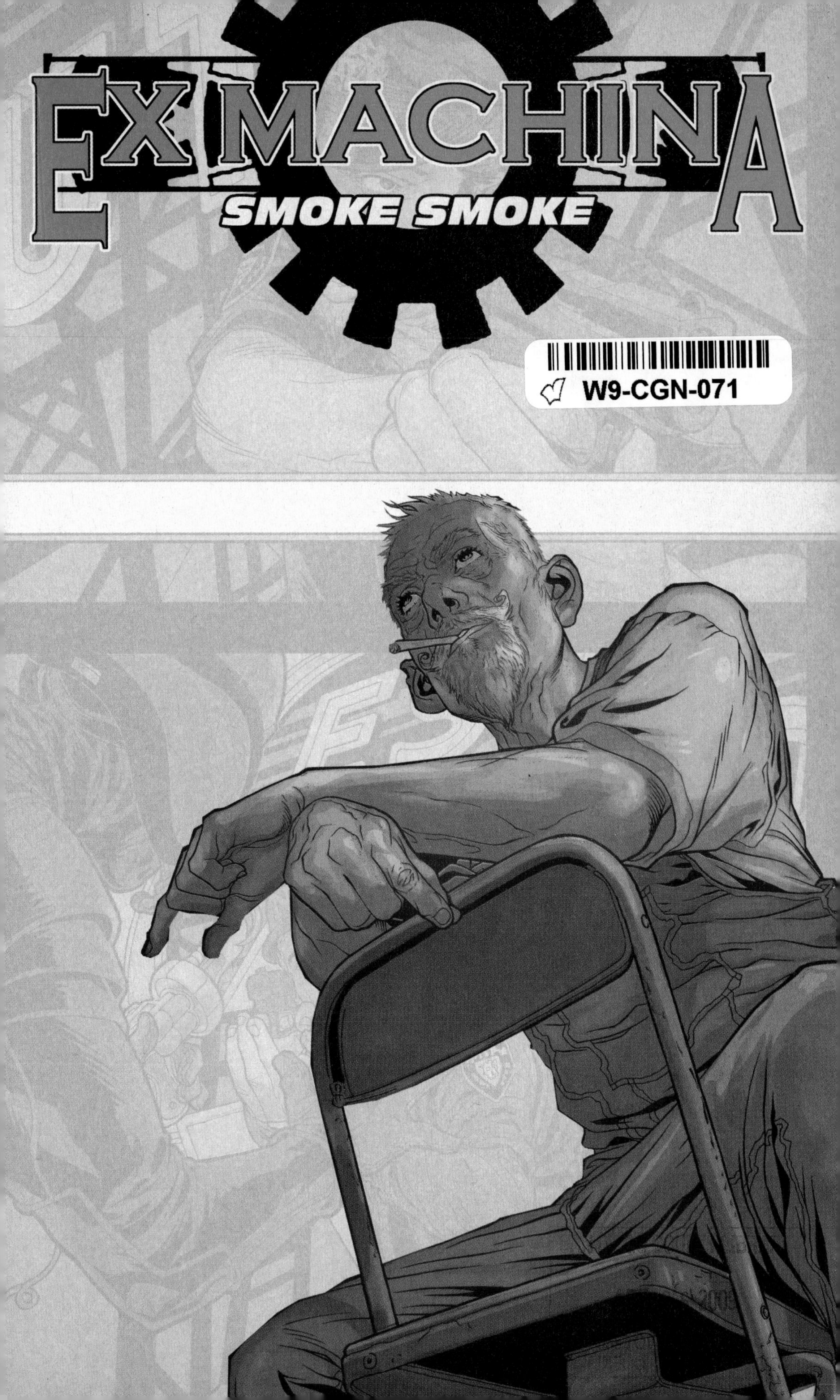
EX MACHINA
SMOKE SMOKE

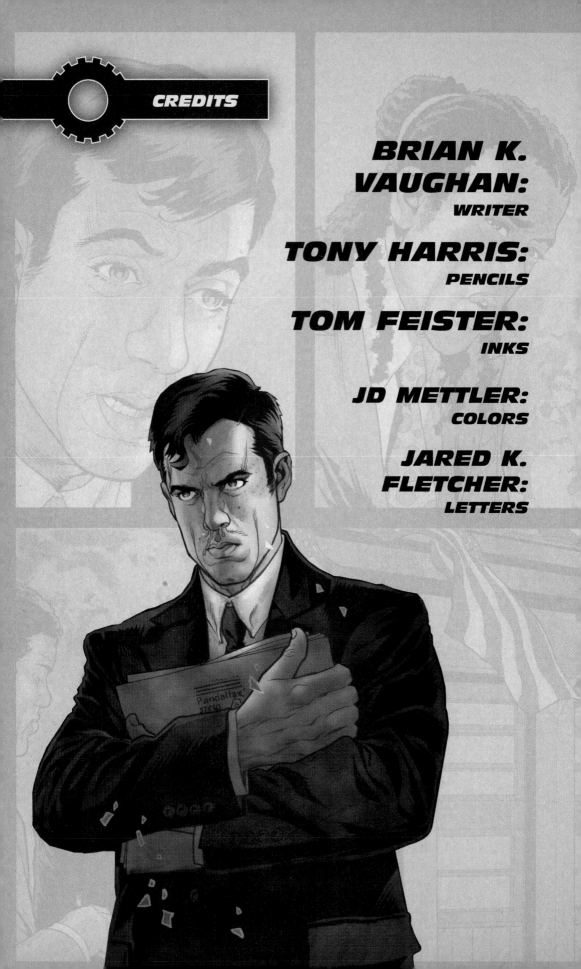

CREDITS

BRIAN K. VAUGHAN: WRITER

TONY HARRIS: PENCILS

TOM FEISTER: INKS

JD METTLER: COLORS

JARED K. FLETCHER: LETTERS

LEGAL

EX MACHINA: SMOKE SMOKE. Published by WildStorm Productions, an imprint of DC Comics. 888 Prospect St. #240, La Jolla, CA 92037. Cover, compilation copyright © 2007 Brian K. Vaughan and Tony Harris. All Rights Reserved. EX MACHINA is ™ Brian K. Vaughan and Tony Harris. Originally published in single magazine form as EX MACHINA #21-25 © 2006, 2007 Brian K. Vaughan and Tony Harris.

ISBN: 1-4012-1322-7   ISBN-13: 978-1-4012-1322-0

Chapter 1
Smoke Smoke

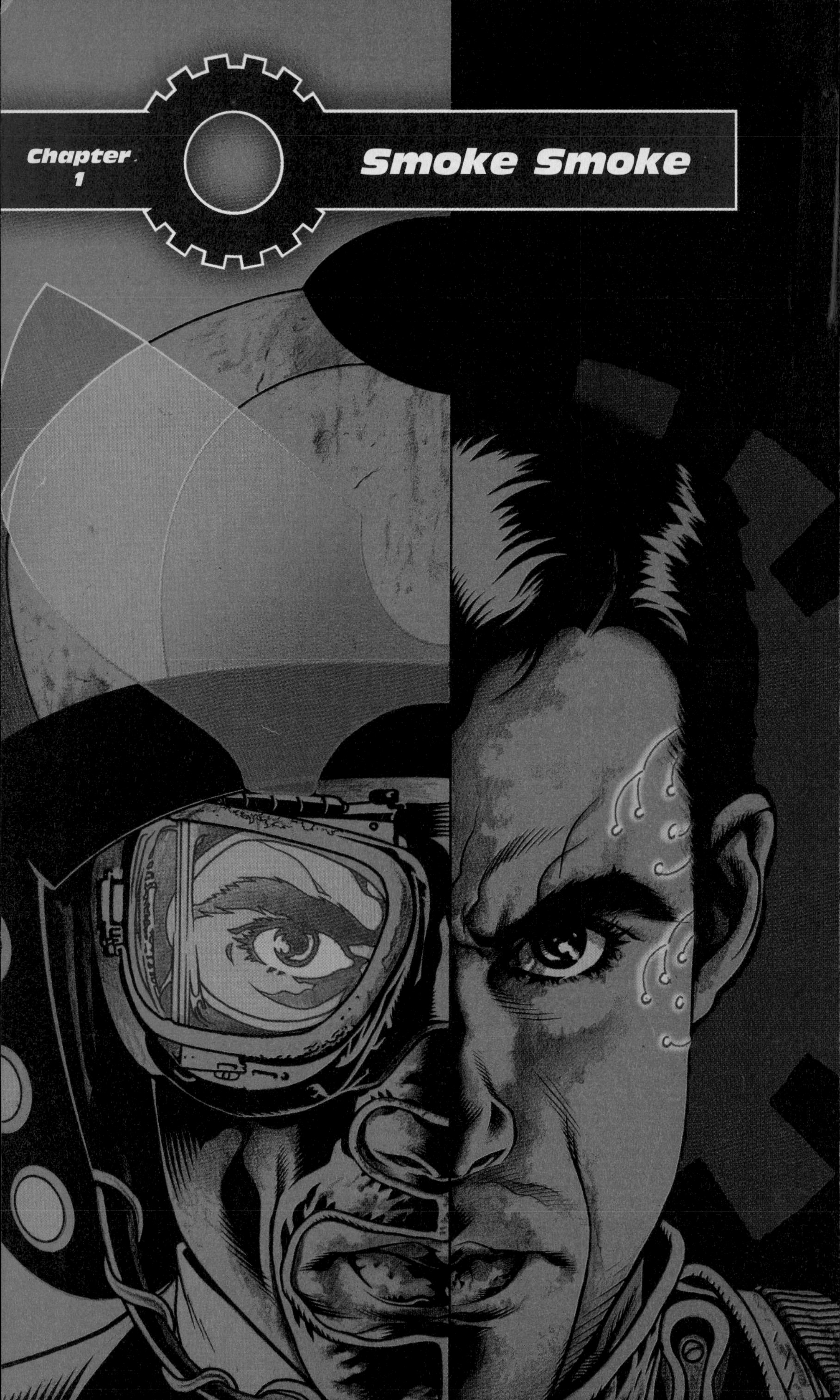

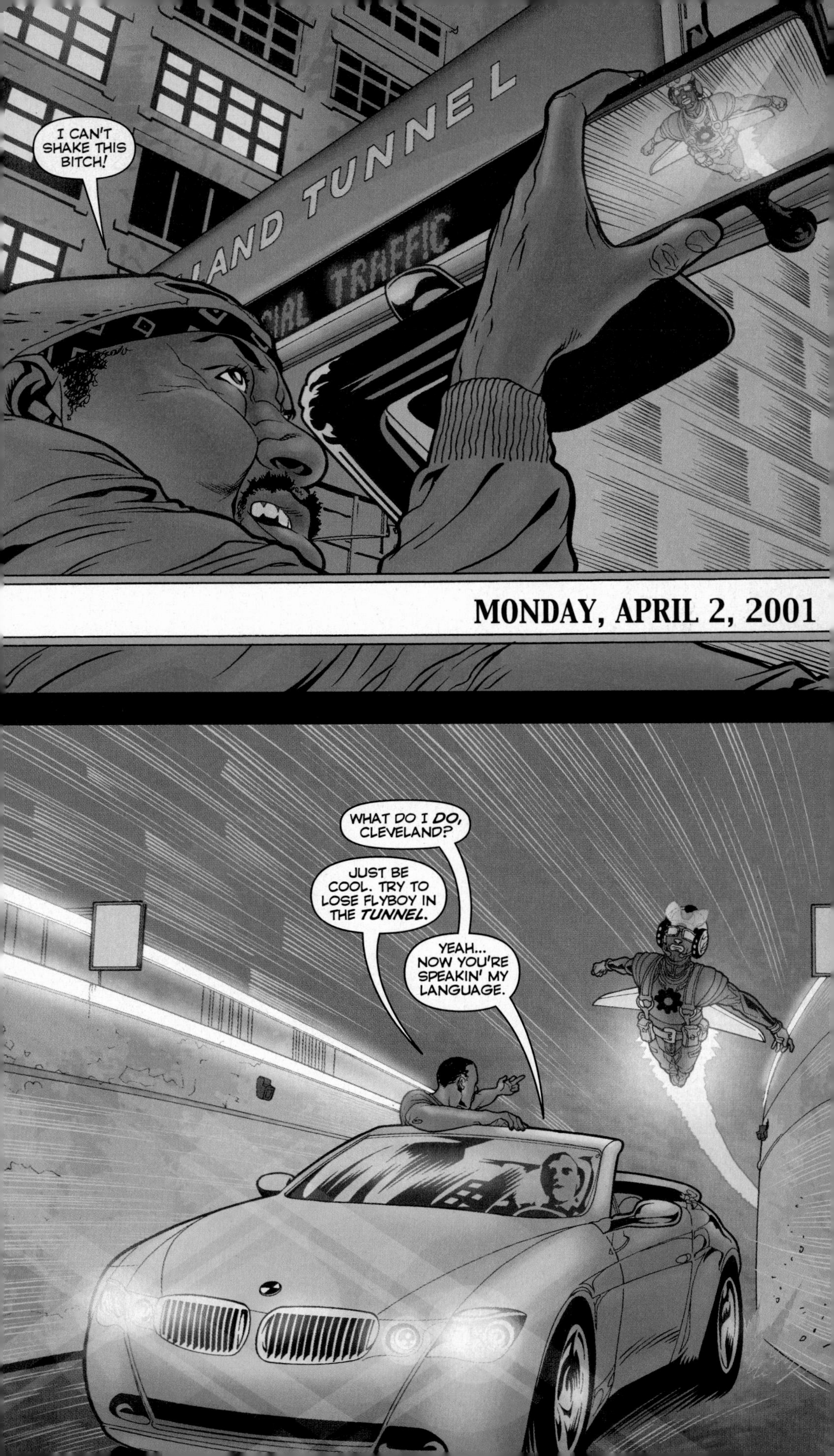
I CAN'T SHAKE THIS BITCH!
LAND TUNNEL
MONDAY, APRIL 2, 2001
WHAT DO I *DO*, CLEVELAND?
JUST BE COOL. TRY TO LOSE FLYBOY IN THE *TUNNEL*.
YEAH... NOW YOU'RE SPEAKIN' MY LANGUAGE.

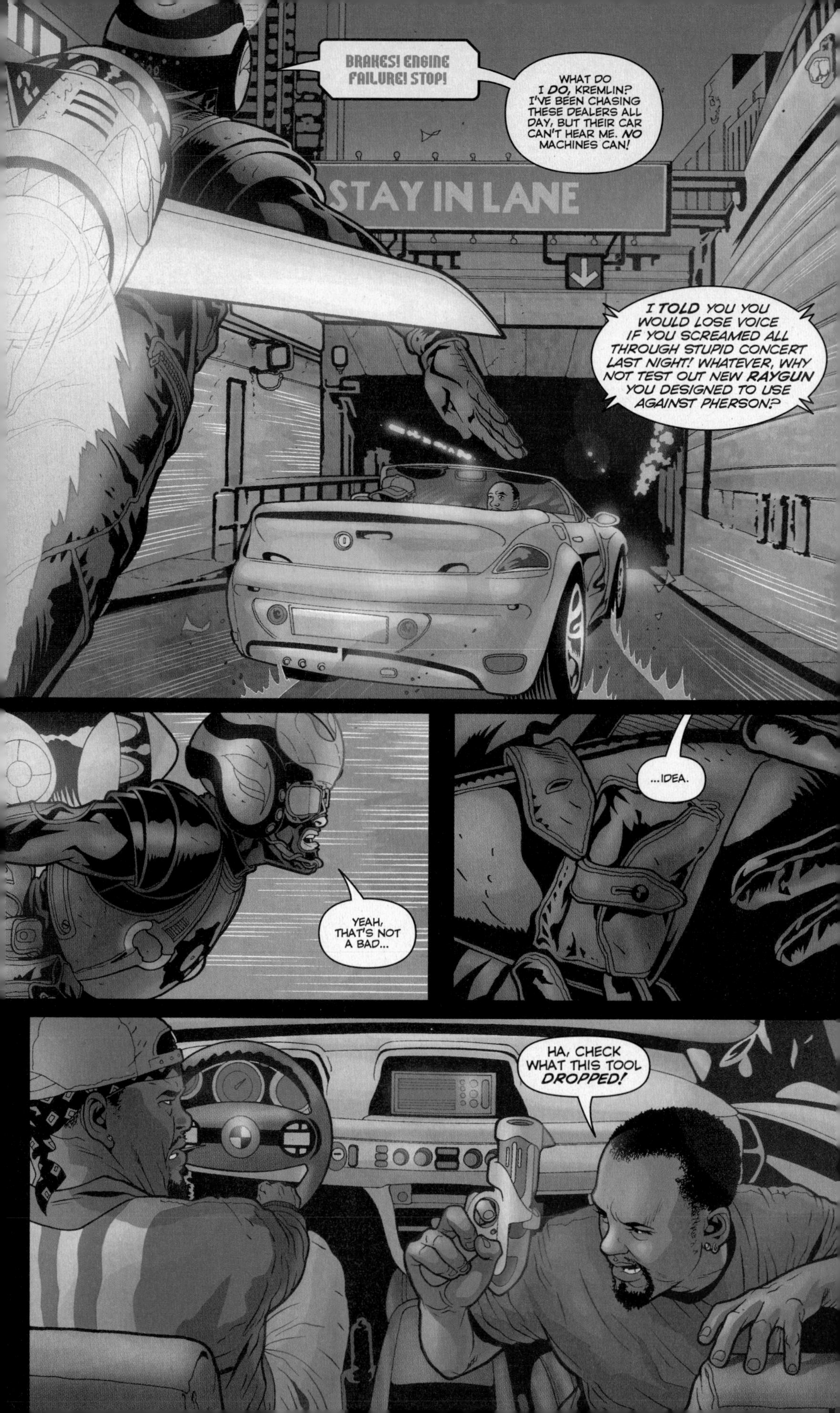
BRAKES! ENGINE FAILURE! STOP!
WHAT DO I DO, KREMLIN? I'VE BEEN CHASING THESE DEALERS ALL DAY, BUT THEIR CAR CAN'T HEAR ME. NO MACHINES CAN!
STAY IN LANE
I TOLD YOU YOU WOULD LOSE VOICE IF YOU SCREAMED ALL THROUGH STUPID CONCERT LAST NIGHT! WHATEVER, WHY NOT TEST OUT NEW RAYGUN YOU DESIGNED TO USE AGAINST PHERSON?
YEAH, THAT'S NOT A BAD...
...IDEA.
HA, CHECK WHAT THIS TOOL DROPPED!

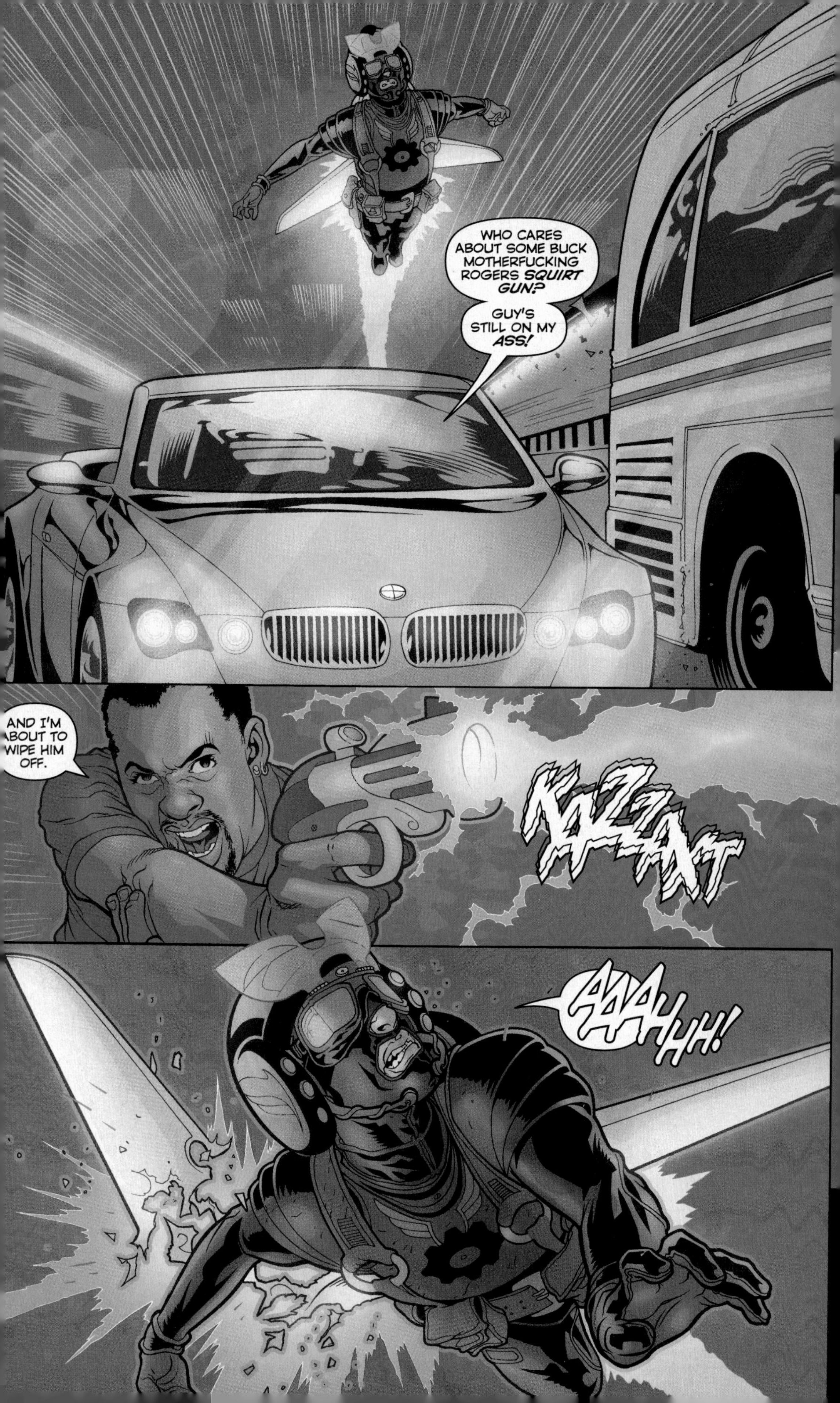

WHO CARES ABOUT SOME BUCK MOTHERFUCKING ROGERS SQUIRT GUN?
GUY'S STILL ON MY ASS!
AND I'M ABOUT TO WIPE HIM OFF.
KAZZAAT
AAAAAHHH!

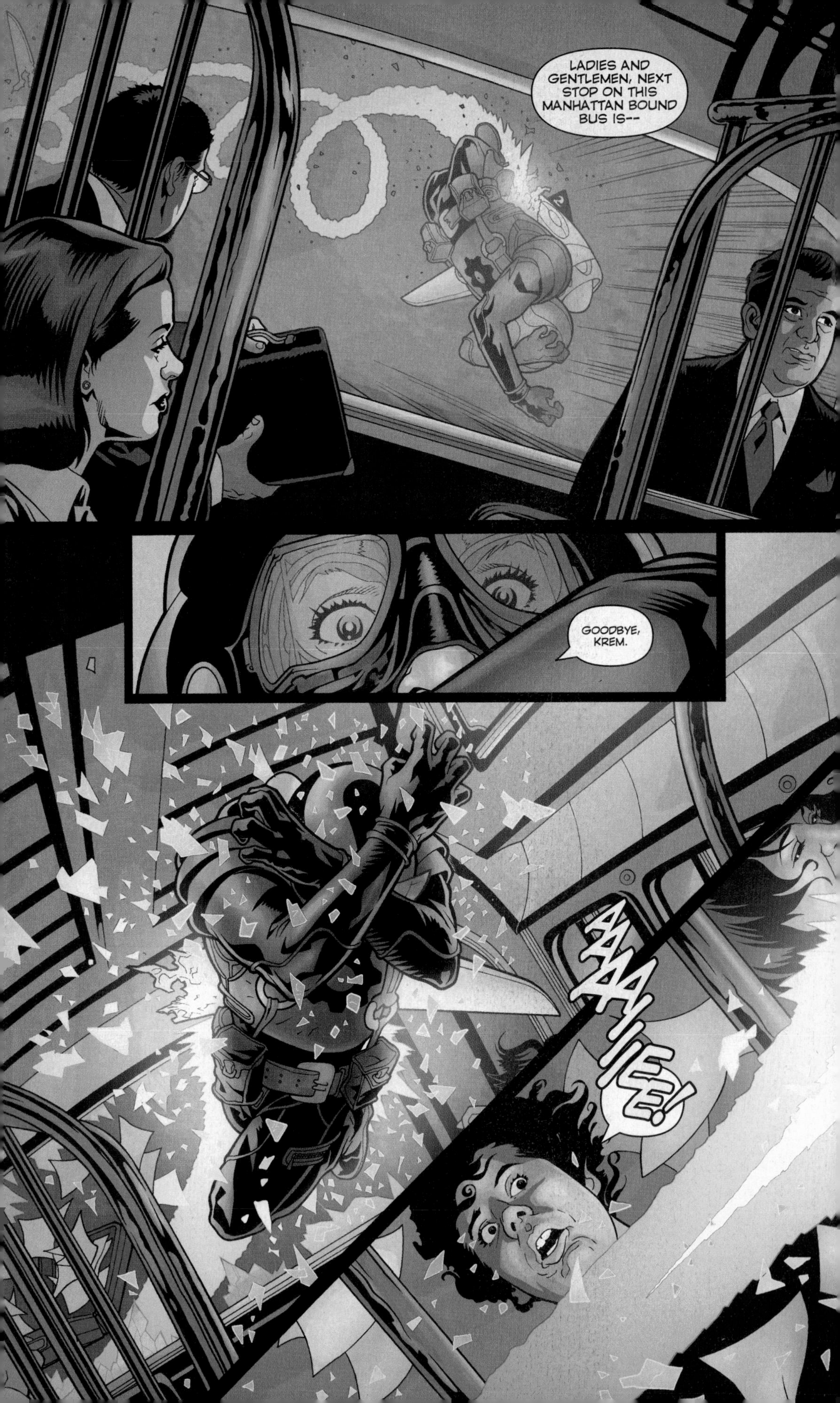
LADIES AND GENTLEMEN, NEXT STOP ON THIS MANHATTAN BOUND BUS IS--
GOODBYE, KREM.
AAAAIIIEE!

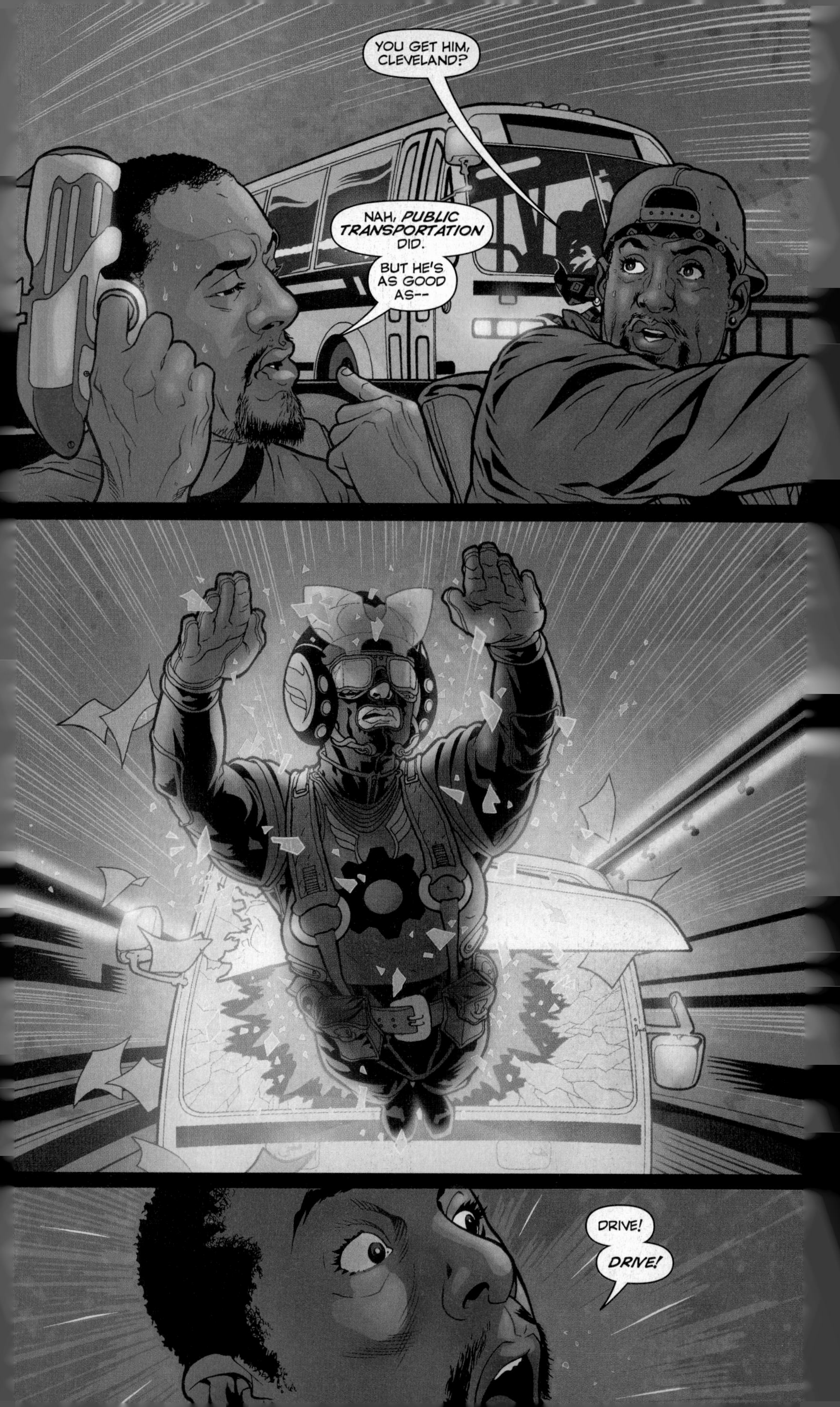
YOU GET HIM, CLEVELAND?
NAH, *PUBLIC TRANSPORTATION* DID.
BUT HE'S AS GOOD AS--
DRIVE!
DRIVE!

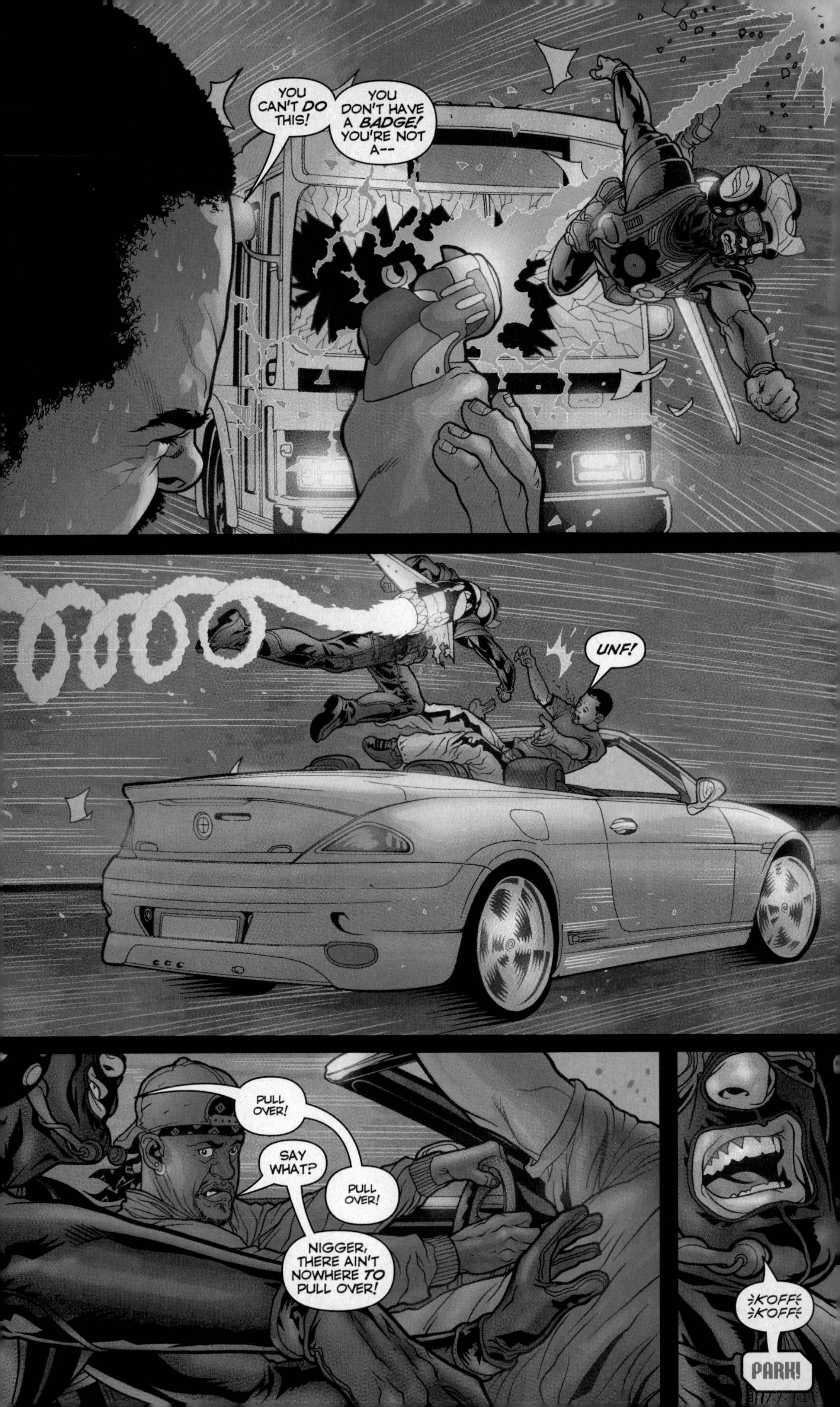

YOU CAN'T *DO* THIS!
YOU DON'T HAVE A *BADGE!* YOU'RE NOT A--
UNF!
PULL OVER!
SAY WHAT?
PULL OVER!
NIGGER, THERE AIN'T NOWHERE *TO* PULL OVER!
KOFF KOFF
PARK!

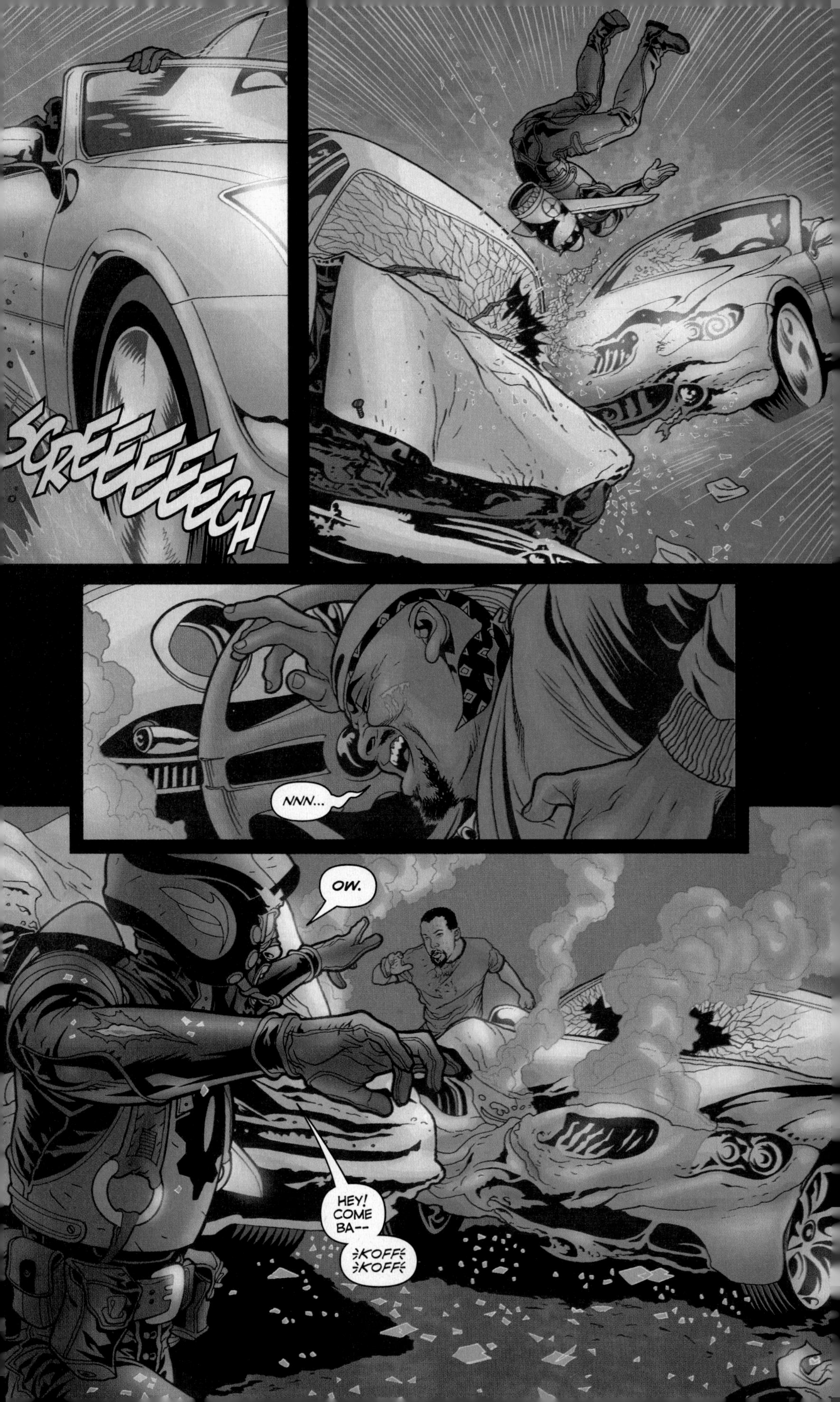
SCREEEEEEECH
NNN...
OW.
HEY! COME BA--
KOFF KOFF

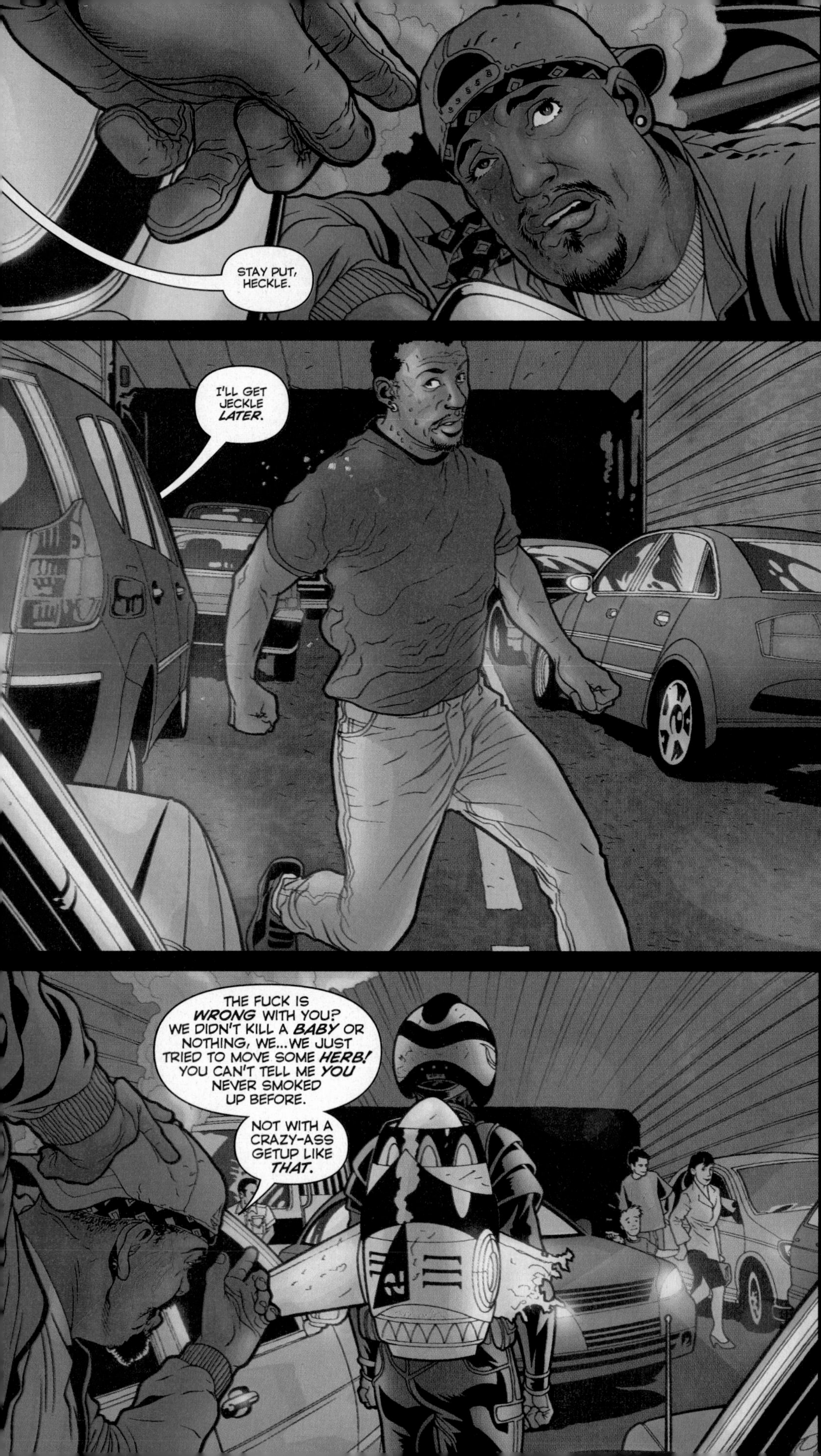
STAY PUT, HECKLE.
I'LL GET JECKLE LATER.
THE FUCK IS WRONG WITH YOU? WE DIDN'T KILL A BABY OR NOTHING, WE...WE JUST TRIED TO MOVE SOME HERB! YOU CAN'T TELL ME YOU NEVER SMOKED UP BEFORE.
NOT WITH A CRAZY-ASS GETUP LIKE THAT.

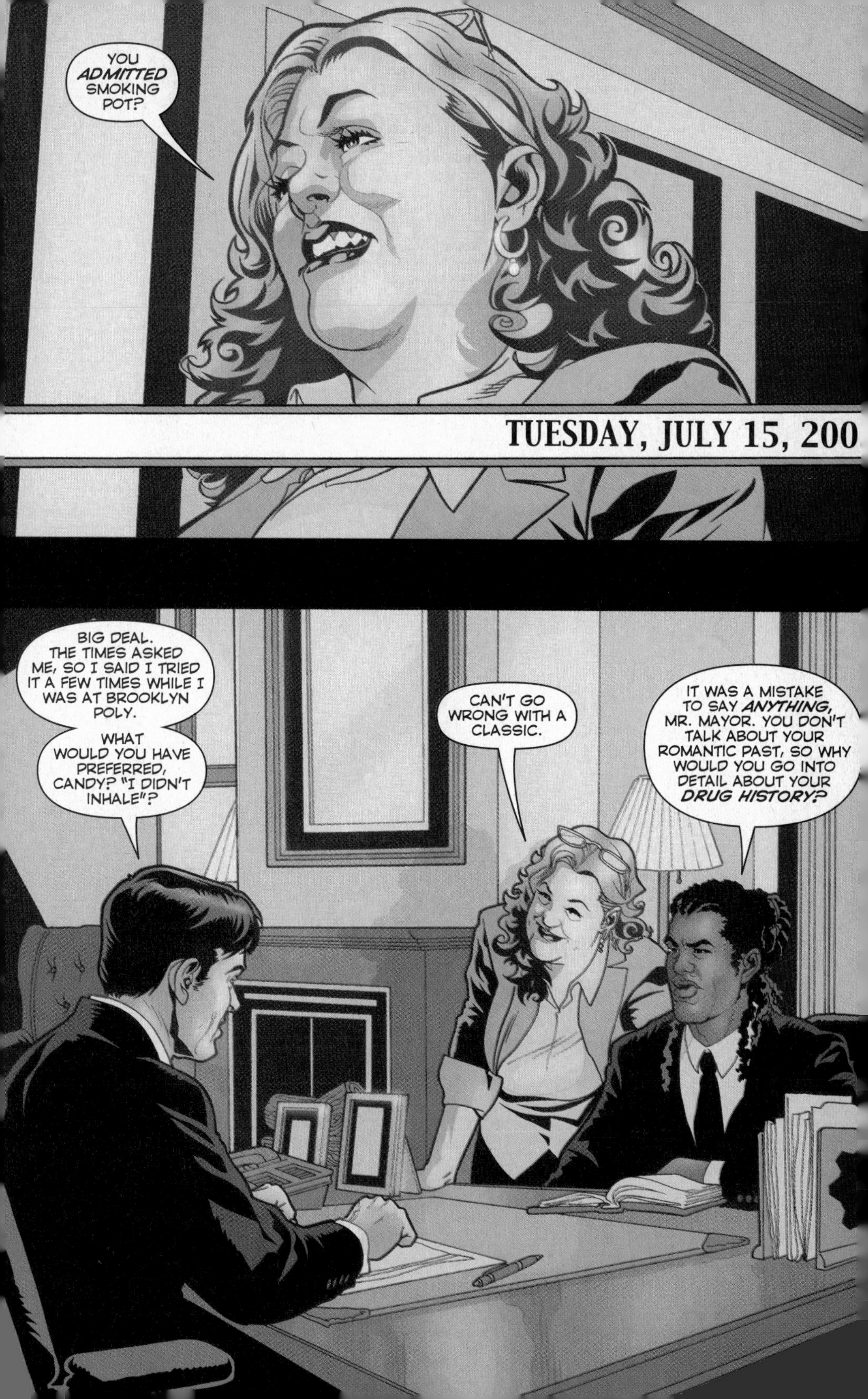
YOU ADMITTED SMOKING POT?
TUESDAY, JULY 15, 200
BIG DEAL. THE TIMES ASKED ME, SO I SAID I TRIED IT A FEW TIMES WHILE I WAS AT BROOKLYN POLY.
WHAT WOULD YOU HAVE PREFERRED, CANDY? "I DIDN'T INHALE"?
CAN'T GO WRONG WITH A CLASSIC.
IT WAS A MISTAKE TO SAY ANYTHING, MR. MAYOR. YOU DON'T TALK ABOUT YOUR ROMANTIC PAST, SO WHY WOULD YOU GO INTO DETAIL ABOUT YOUR DRUG HISTORY?

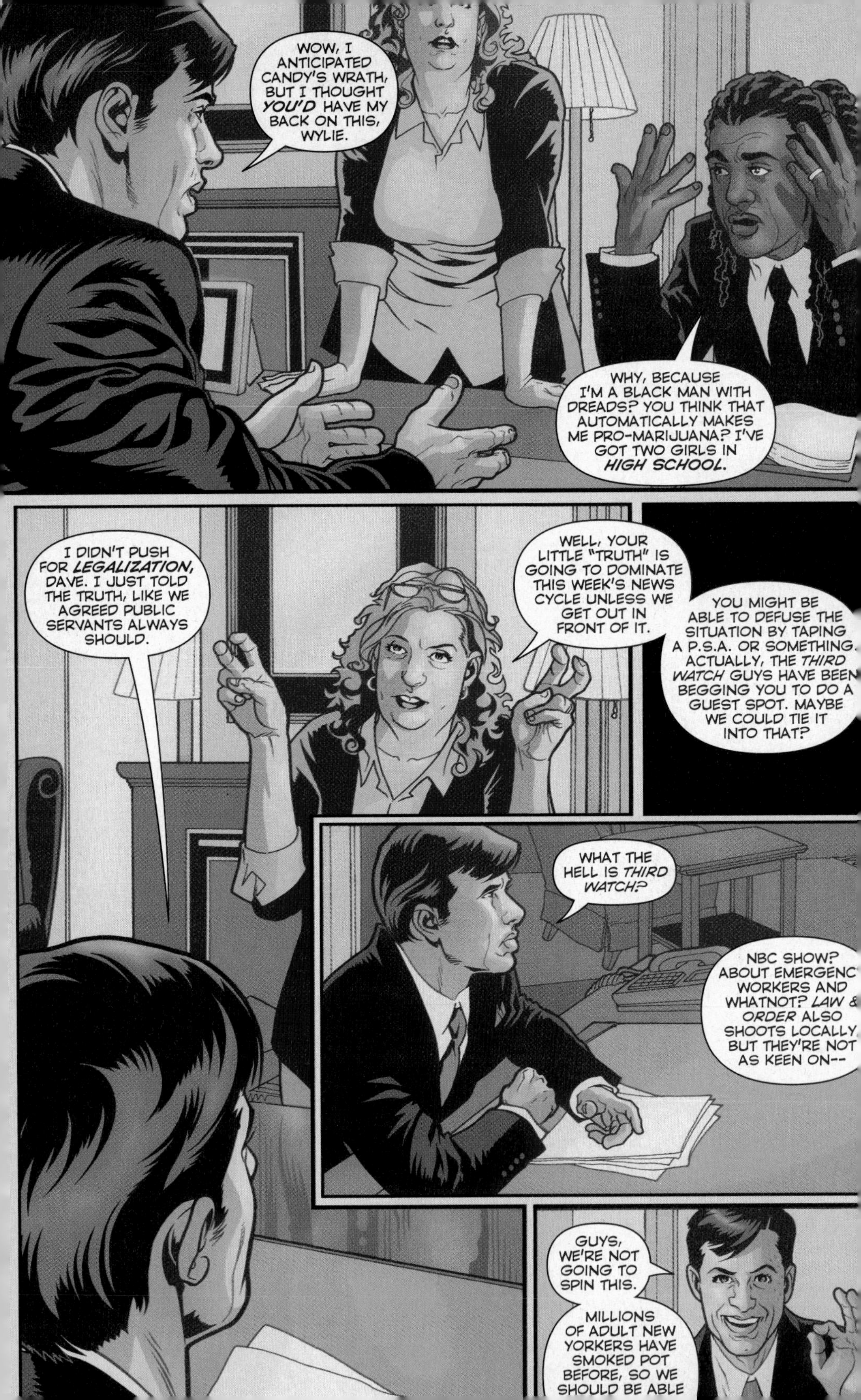

WOW, I ANTICIPATED CANDY'S WRATH, BUT I THOUGHT *YOU'D* HAVE MY BACK ON THIS, WYLIE.
WHY, BECAUSE I'M A BLACK MAN WITH DREADS? YOU THINK THAT AUTOMATICALLY MAKES ME PRO-MARIJUANA? I'VE GOT TWO GIRLS IN ***HIGH SCHOOL.***
I DIDN'T PUSH FOR ***LEGALIZATION,*** DAVE. I JUST TOLD THE TRUTH, LIKE WE AGREED PUBLIC SERVANTS ALWAYS SHOULD.
WELL, YOUR LITTLE "TRUTH" IS GOING TO DOMINATE THIS WEEK'S NEWS CYCLE UNLESS WE GET OUT IN FRONT OF IT.
YOU MIGHT BE ABLE TO DEFUSE THE SITUATION BY TAPING A P.S.A. OR SOMETHING. ACTUALLY, THE *THIRD WATCH* GUYS HAVE BEEN BEGGING YOU TO DO A GUEST SPOT. MAYBE WE COULD TIE IT INTO THAT?
WHAT THE HELL IS *THIRD WATCH?*
NBC SHOW? ABOUT EMERGENC WORKERS AND WHATNOT? *LAW & ORDER* ALSO SHOOTS LOCALLY, BUT THEY'RE NOT AS KEEN ON--
GUYS, WE'RE NOT GOING TO SPIN THIS.
MILLIONS OF ADULT NEW YORKERS HAVE SMOKED POT BEFORE, SO WE SHOULD BE ABLE

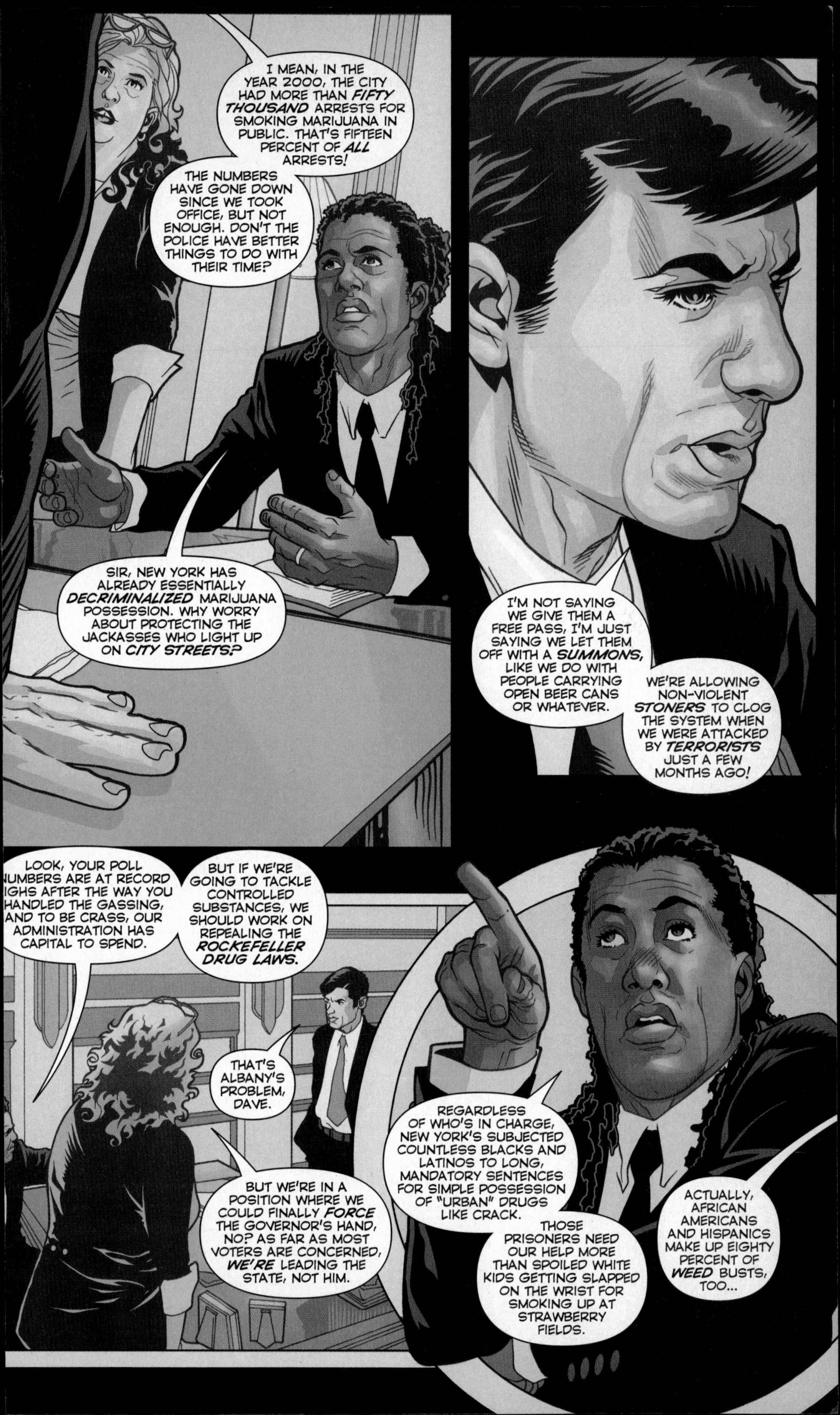
I MEAN, IN THE YEAR 2000, THE CITY HAD MORE THAN FIFTY THOUSAND ARRESTS FOR SMOKING MARIJUANA IN PUBLIC. THAT'S FIFTEEN PERCENT OF ALL ARRESTS!
THE NUMBERS HAVE GONE DOWN SINCE WE TOOK OFFICE, BUT NOT ENOUGH. DON'T THE POLICE HAVE BETTER THINGS TO DO WITH THEIR TIME?
SIR, NEW YORK HAS ALREADY ESSENTIALLY DECRIMINALIZED MARIJUANA POSSESSION. WHY WORRY ABOUT PROTECTING THE JACKASSES WHO LIGHT UP ON CITY STREETS?
I'M NOT SAYING WE GIVE THEM A FREE PASS, I'M JUST SAYING WE LET THEM OFF WITH A SUMMONS, LIKE WE DO WITH PEOPLE CARRYING OPEN BEER CANS OR WHATEVER.
WE'RE ALLOWING NON-VIOLENT STONERS TO CLOG THE SYSTEM WHEN WE WERE ATTACKED BY TERRORISTS JUST A FEW MONTHS AGO!
LOOK, YOUR POLL NUMBERS ARE AT RECORD HIGHS AFTER THE WAY YOU HANDLED THE GASSING, AND TO BE CRASS, OUR ADMINISTRATION HAS CAPITAL TO SPEND.
BUT IF WE'RE GOING TO TACKLE CONTROLLED SUBSTANCES, WE SHOULD WORK ON REPEALING THE ROCKEFELLER DRUG LAWS.
THAT'S ALBANY'S PROBLEM, DAVE.
BUT WE'RE IN A POSITION WHERE WE COULD FINALLY FORCE THE GOVERNOR'S HAND, NO? AS FAR AS MOST VOTERS ARE CONCERNED, WE'RE LEADING THE STATE, NOT HIM.
REGARDLESS OF WHO'S IN CHARGE, NEW YORK'S SUBJECTED COUNTLESS BLACKS AND LATINOS TO LONG, MANDATORY SENTENCES FOR SIMPLE POSSESSION OF "URBAN" DRUGS LIKE CRACK.
THOSE PRISONERS NEED OUR HELP MORE THAN SPOILED WHITE KIDS GETTING SLAPPED ON THE WRIST FOR SMOKING UP AT STRAWBERRY FIELDS.
ACTUALLY, AFRICAN AMERICANS AND HISPANICS MAKE UP EIGHTY PERCENT OF WEED BUSTS, TOO...

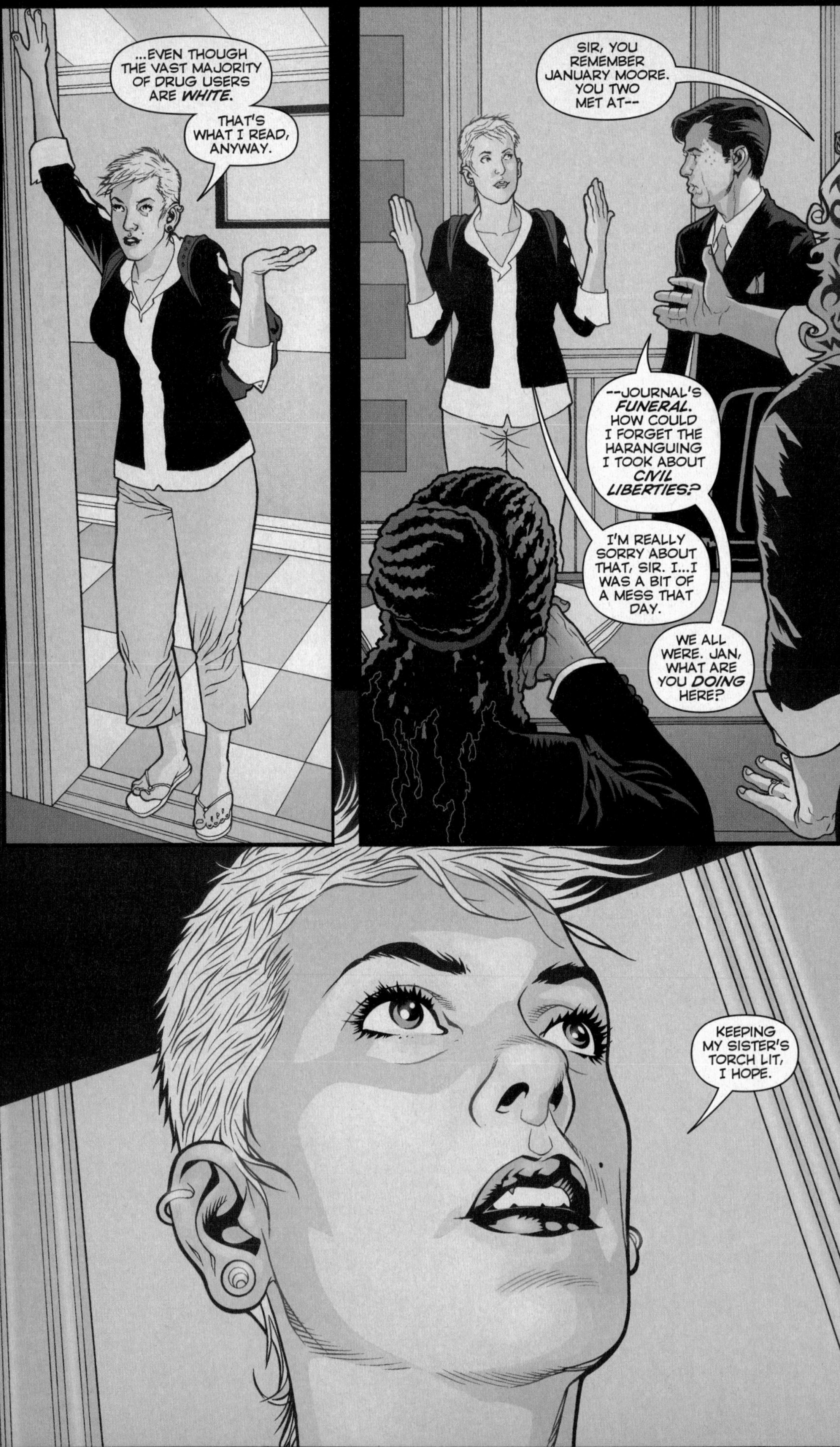
...EVEN THOUGH THE VAST MAJORITY OF DRUG USERS ARE *WHITE*.
THAT'S WHAT I READ, ANYWAY.
SIR, YOU REMEMBER JANUARY MOORE. YOU TWO MET AT--
--JOURNAL'S *FUNERAL*. HOW COULD I FORGET THE HARANGUING I TOOK ABOUT *CIVIL LIBERTIES?*
I'M REALLY SORRY ABOUT THAT, SIR. I...I WAS A BIT OF A MESS THAT DAY.
WE ALL WERE. JAN, WHAT ARE YOU *DOING* HERE?
KEEPING MY SISTER'S TORCH LIT, I HOPE.

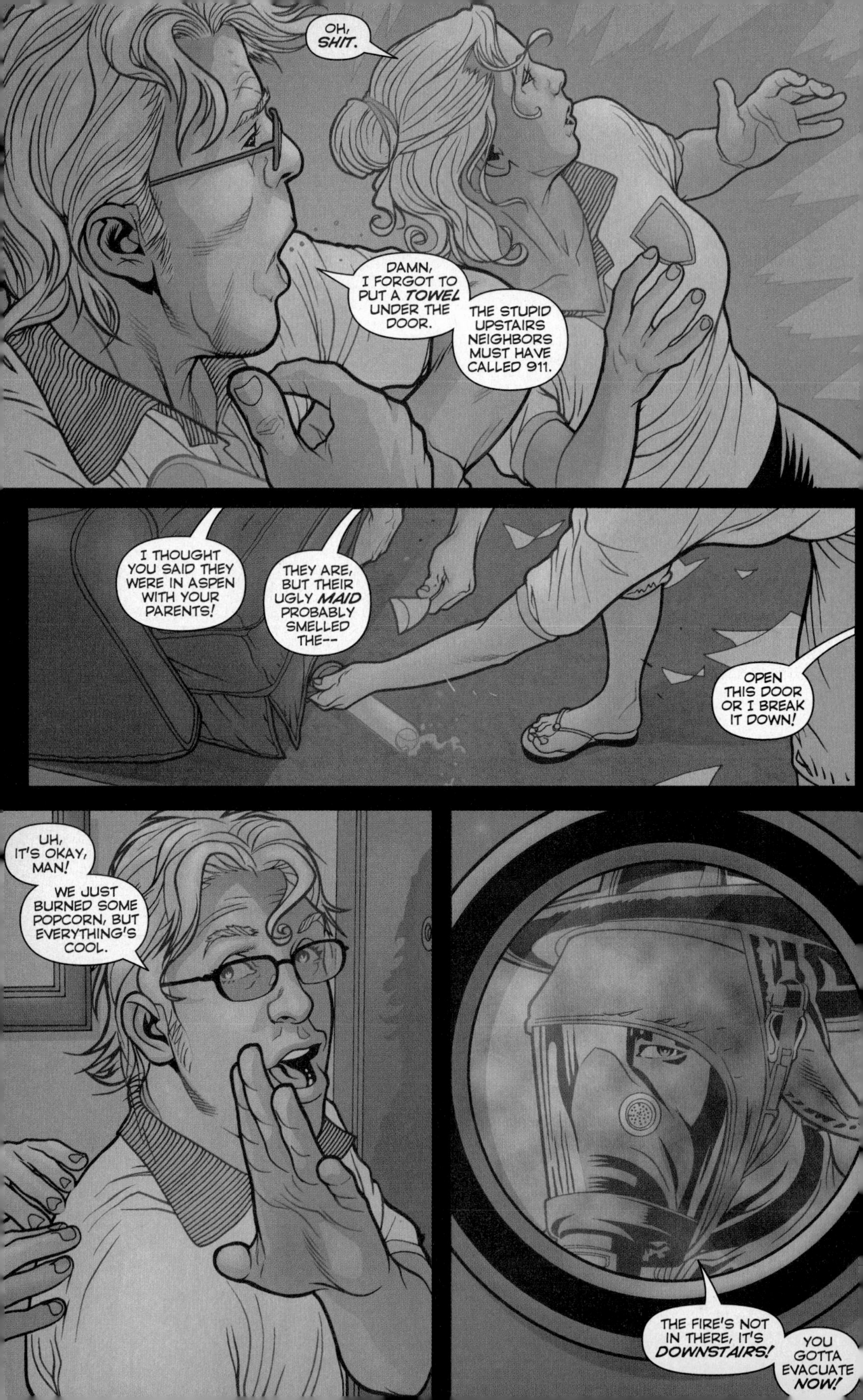
OH, *SHIT*.
DAMN, I FORGOT TO PUT A *TOWEL* UNDER THE DOOR.
THE STUPID UPSTAIRS NEIGHBORS MUST HAVE CALLED 911.
I THOUGHT YOU SAID THEY WERE IN ASPEN WITH YOUR PARENTS!
THEY ARE, BUT THEIR UGLY *MAID* PROBABLY SMELLED THE--
OPEN THIS DOOR OR I BREAK IT DOWN!
UH, IT'S OKAY, MAN!
WE JUST BURNED SOME POPCORN, BUT EVERYTHING'S COOL.
THE FIRE'S NOT IN THERE, IT'S *DOWNSTAIRS!*
YOU GOTTA EVACUATE *NOW!*

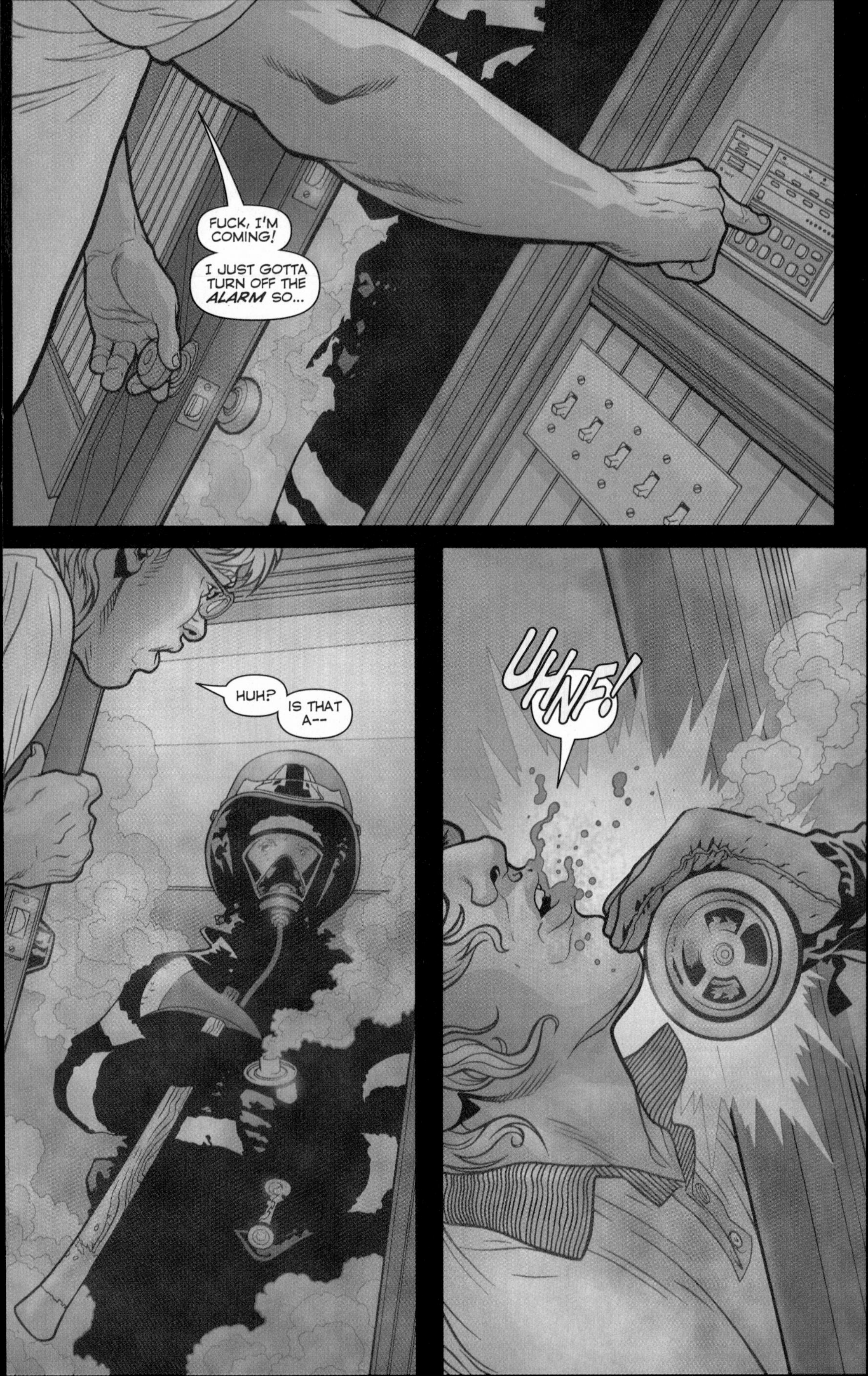
FUCK, I'M COMING!
I JUST GOTTA TURN OFF THE *ALARM* SO...
HUH?
IS THAT A--
UHNF!

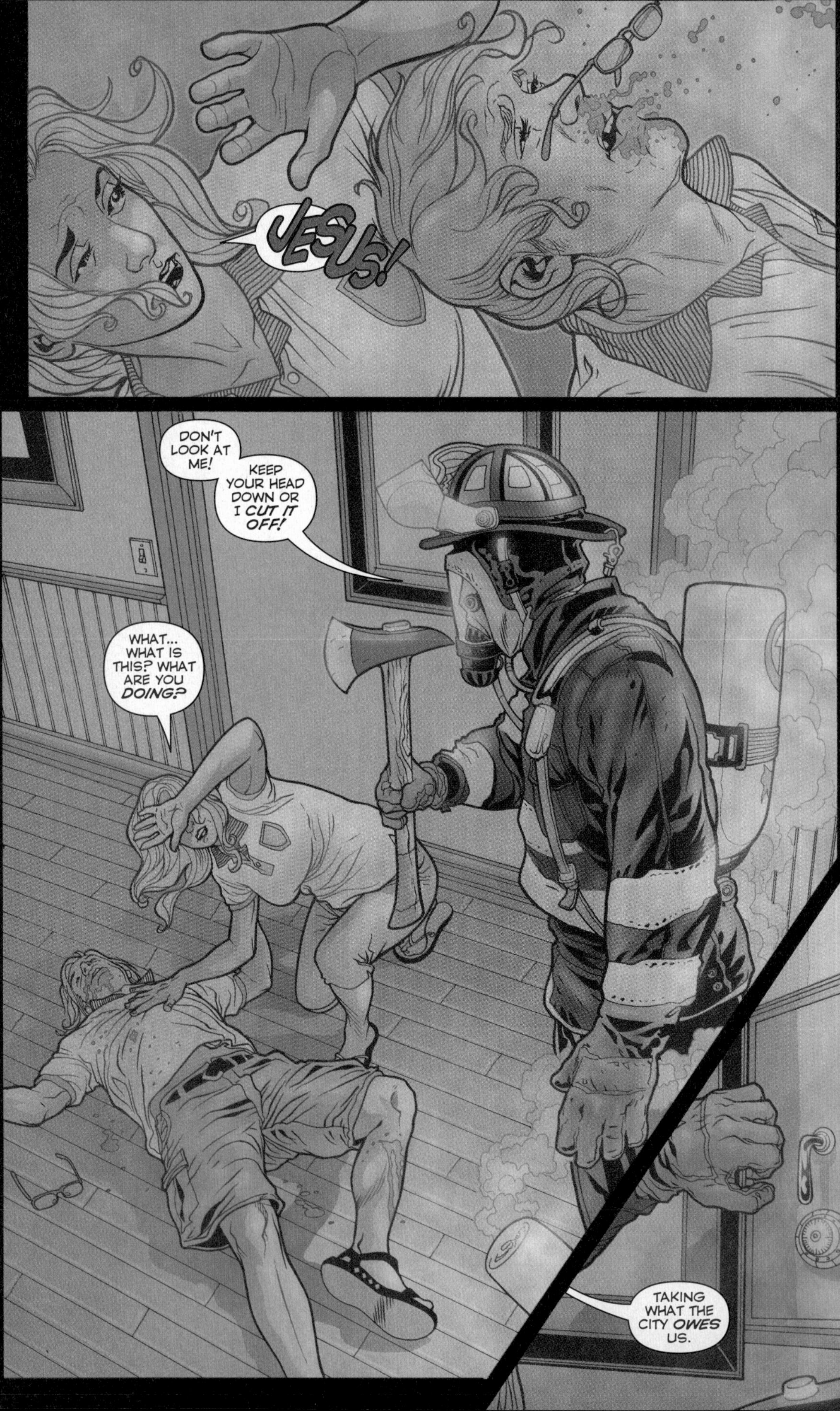

JESUS!
DON'T LOOK AT ME!
KEEP YOUR HEAD DOWN OR I CUT IT OFF!
WHAT... WHAT IS THIS? WHAT ARE YOU DOING?
TAKING WHAT THE CITY OWES US.

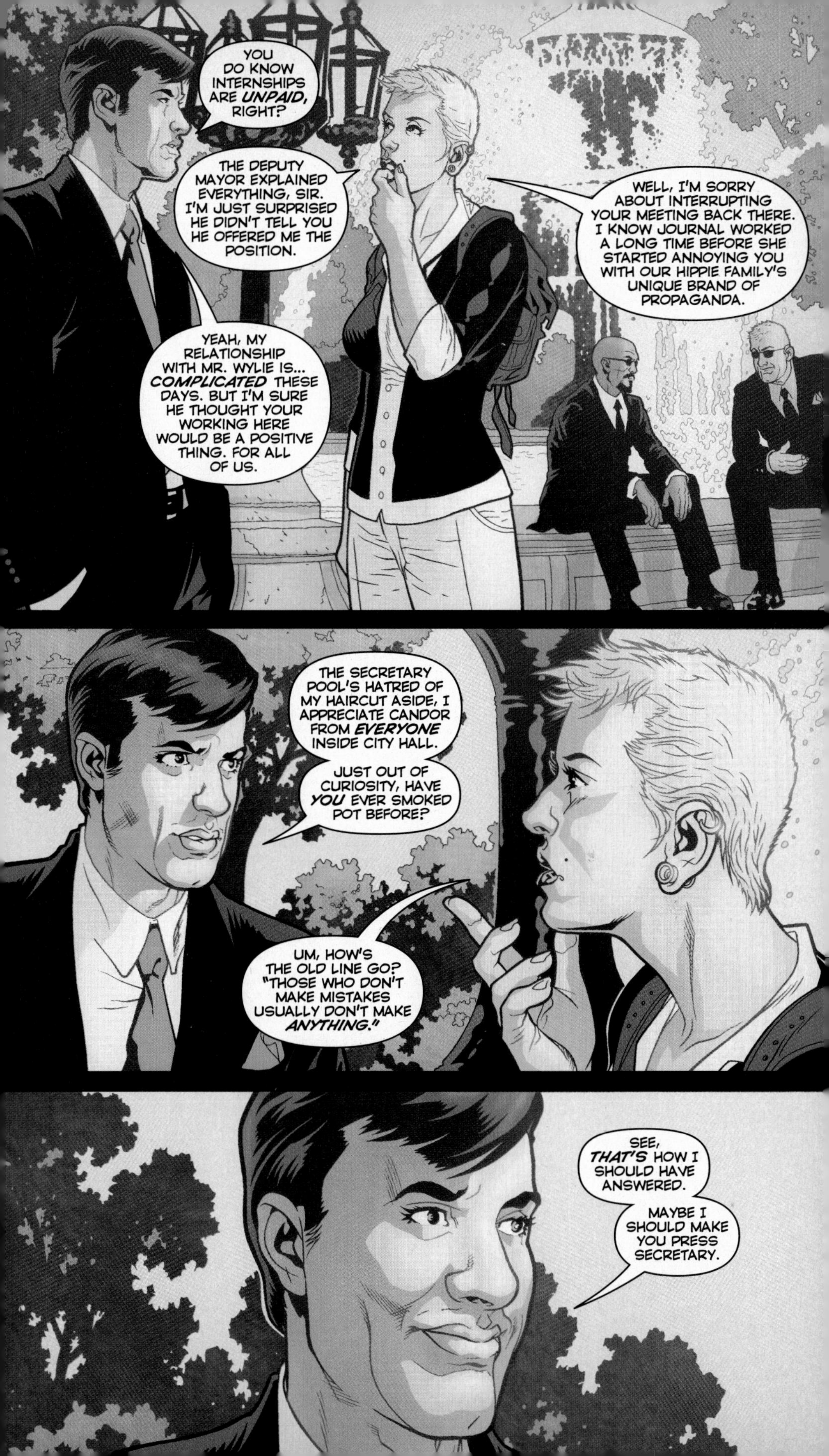

YOU DO KNOW INTERNSHIPS ARE *UNPAID,* RIGHT?
THE DEPUTY MAYOR EXPLAINED EVERYTHING, SIR. I'M JUST SURPRISED HE DIDN'T TELL YOU HE OFFERED ME THE POSITION.
WELL, I'M SORRY ABOUT INTERRUPTING YOUR MEETING BACK THERE. I KNOW JOURNAL WORKED A LONG TIME BEFORE SHE STARTED ANNOYING YOU WITH OUR HIPPIE FAMILY'S UNIQUE BRAND OF PROPAGANDA.
YEAH, MY RELATIONSHIP WITH MR. WYLIE IS... *COMPLICATED* THESE DAYS. BUT I'M SURE HE THOUGHT YOUR WORKING HERE WOULD BE A POSITIVE THING. FOR ALL OF US.
THE SECRETARY POOL'S HATRED OF MY HAIRCUT ASIDE, I APPRECIATE CANDOR FROM *EVERYONE* INSIDE CITY HALL.
JUST OUT OF CURIOSITY, HAVE *YOU* EVER SMOKED POT BEFORE?
UM, HOW'S THE OLD LINE GO? "THOSE WHO DON'T MAKE MISTAKES USUALLY DON'T MAKE *ANYTHING.*"
SEE, *THAT'S* HOW I SHOULD HAVE ANSWERED.
MAYBE I SHOULD MAKE YOU PRESS SECRETARY.

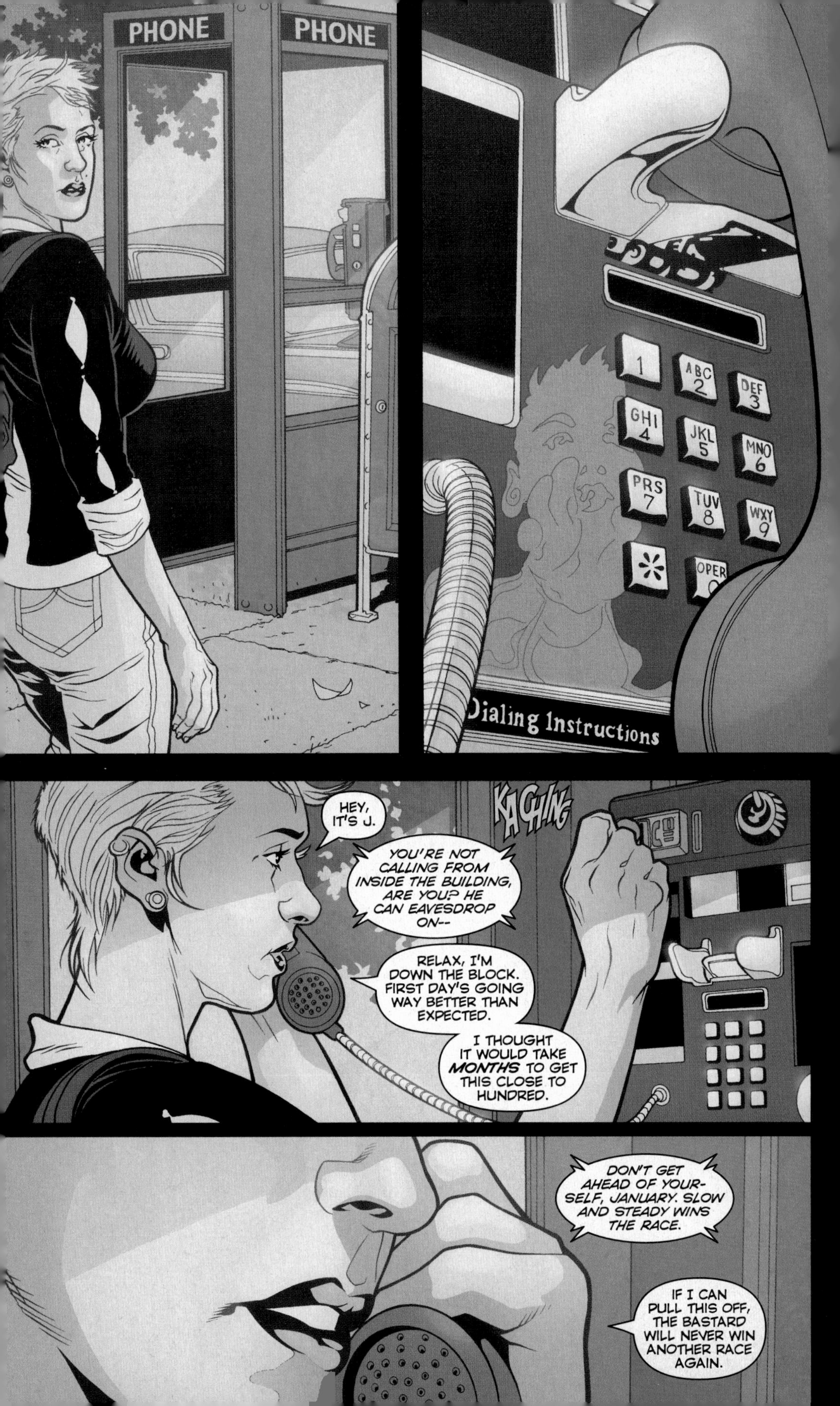
PHONE
PHONE
Dialing Instructions
KACHING
HEY, IT'S J.
YOU'RE NOT CALLING FROM INSIDE THE BUILDING, ARE YOU? HE CAN EAVESDROP ON--
RELAX, I'M DOWN THE BLOCK. FIRST DAY'S GOING WAY BETTER THAN EXPECTED.
I THOUGHT IT WOULD TAKE *MONTHS* TO GET THIS CLOSE TO HUNDRED.
DON'T GET AHEAD OF YOURSELF, JANUARY. SLOW AND STEADY WINS THE RACE.
IF I CAN PULL THIS OFF, THE BASTARD WILL NEVER WIN ANOTHER RACE AGAIN.

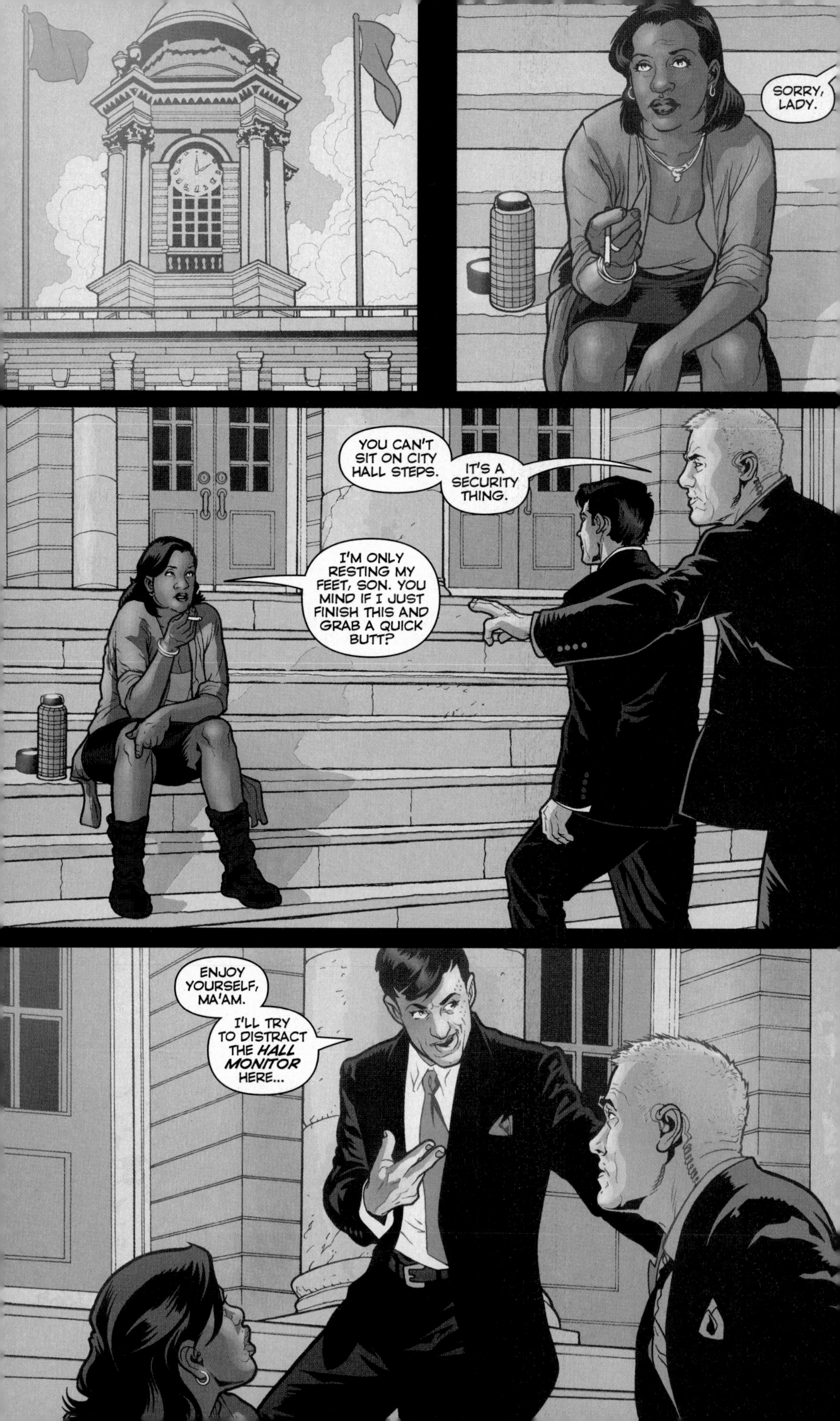
SORRY, LADY.
YOU CAN'T SIT ON CITY HALL STEPS.
IT'S A SECURITY THING.
I'M ONLY RESTING MY FEET, SON. YOU MIND IF I JUST FINISH THIS AND GRAB A QUICK BUTT?
ENJOY YOURSELF, MA'AM.
I'LL TRY TO DISTRACT THE *HALL MONITOR* HERE...

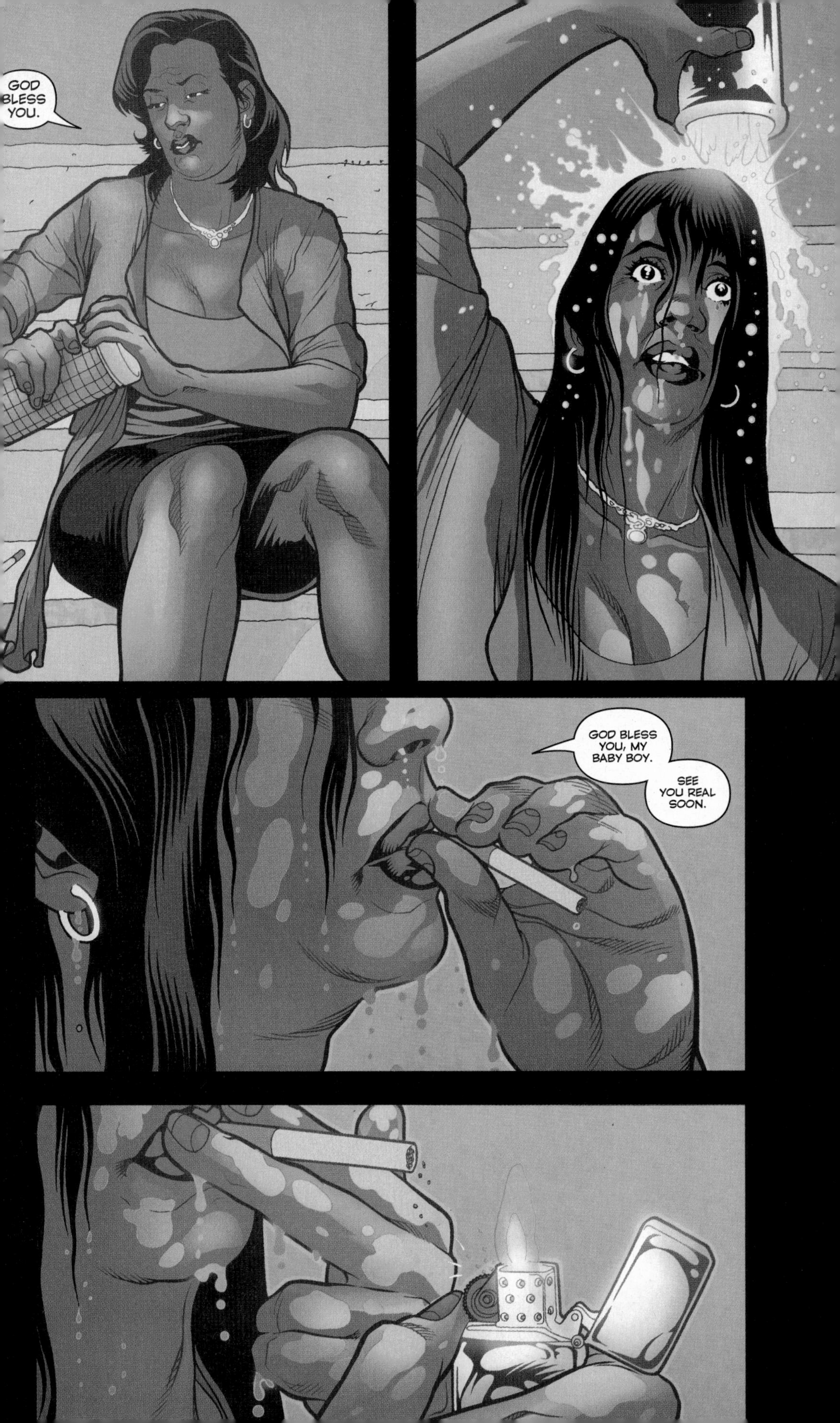
GOD BLESS YOU.
GOD BLESS YOU, MY BABY BOY.
SEE YOU REAL SOON.

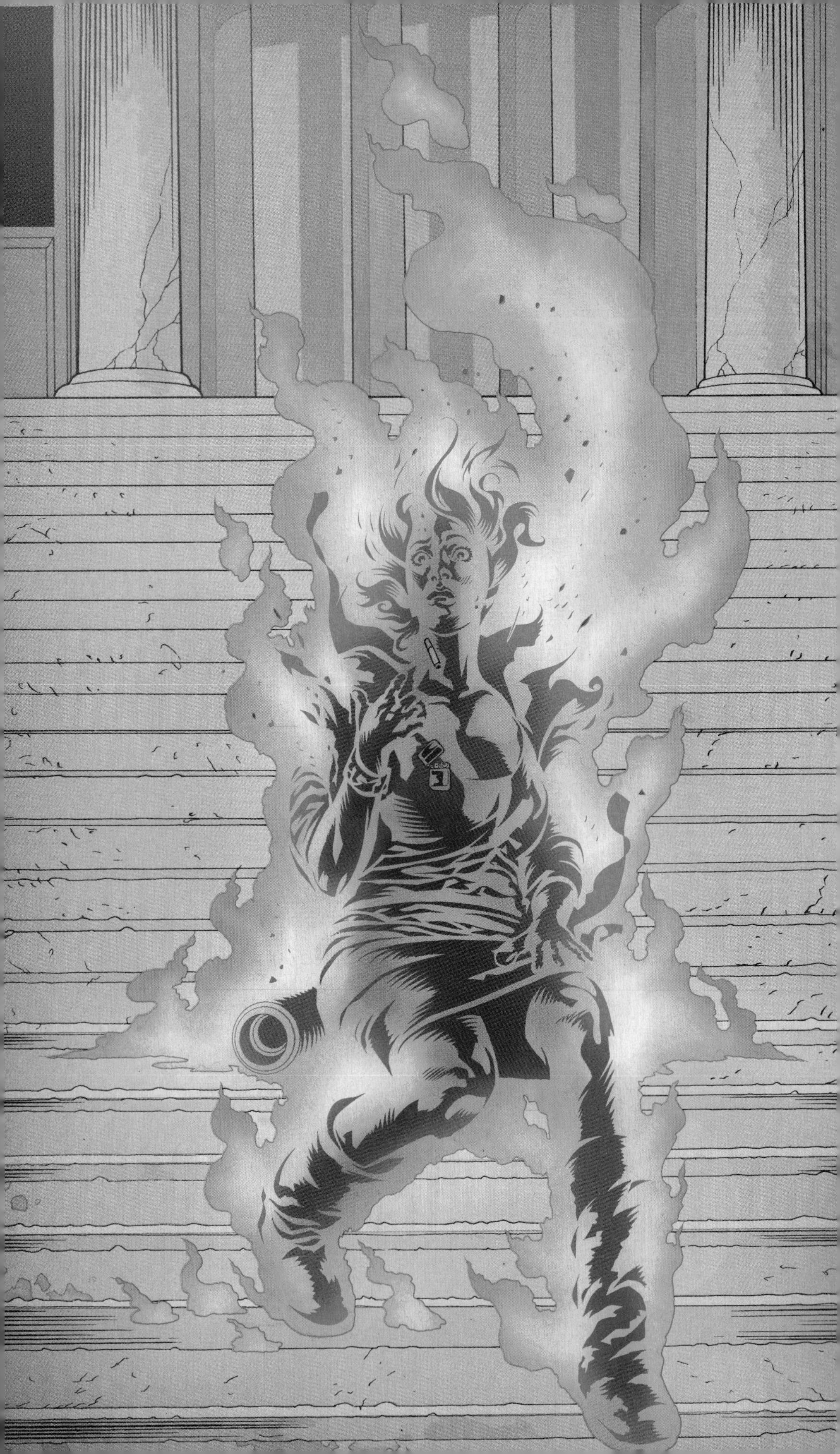

Smoke Smoke

Chapter 2

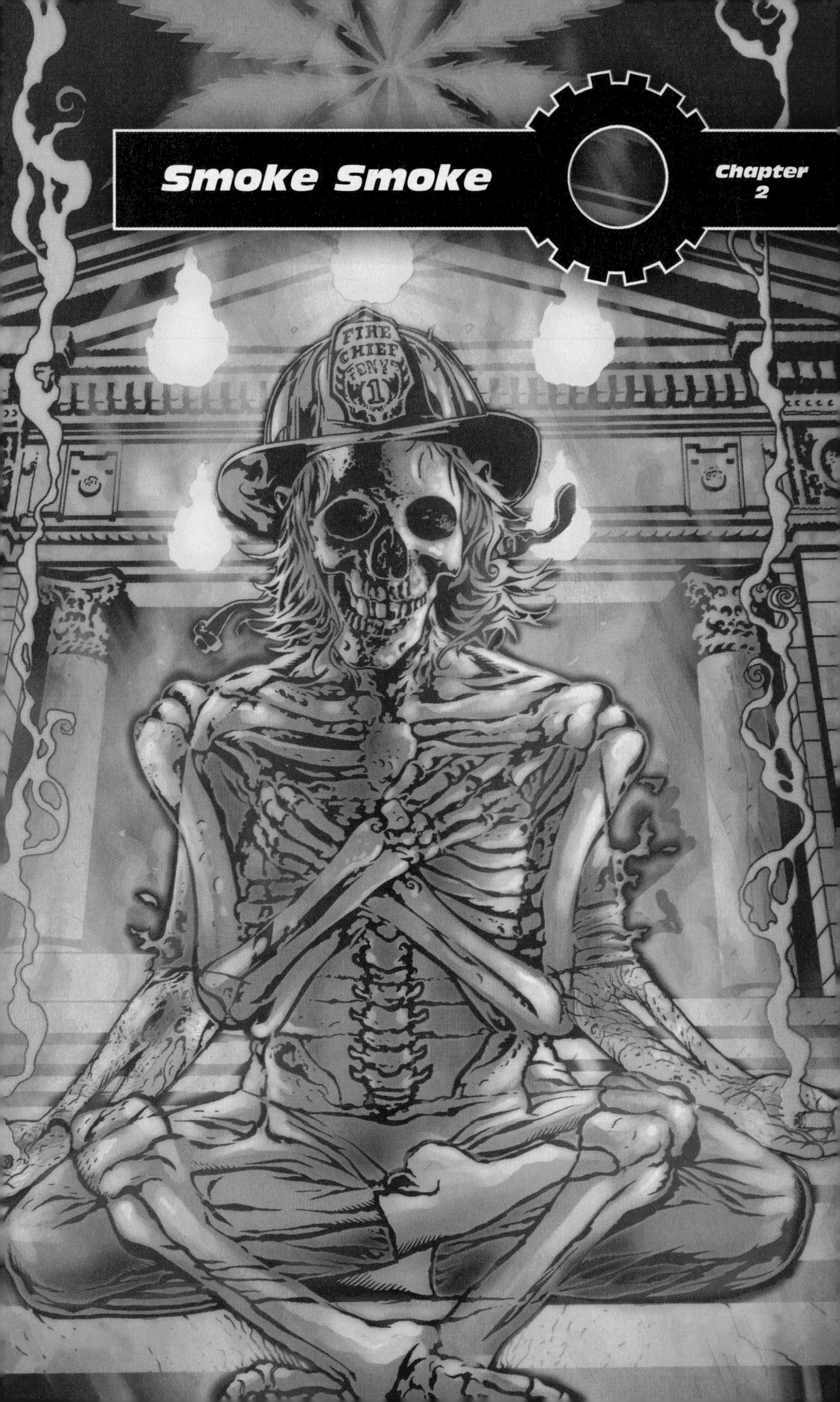
FIRE
CHIEF
FDNY
1

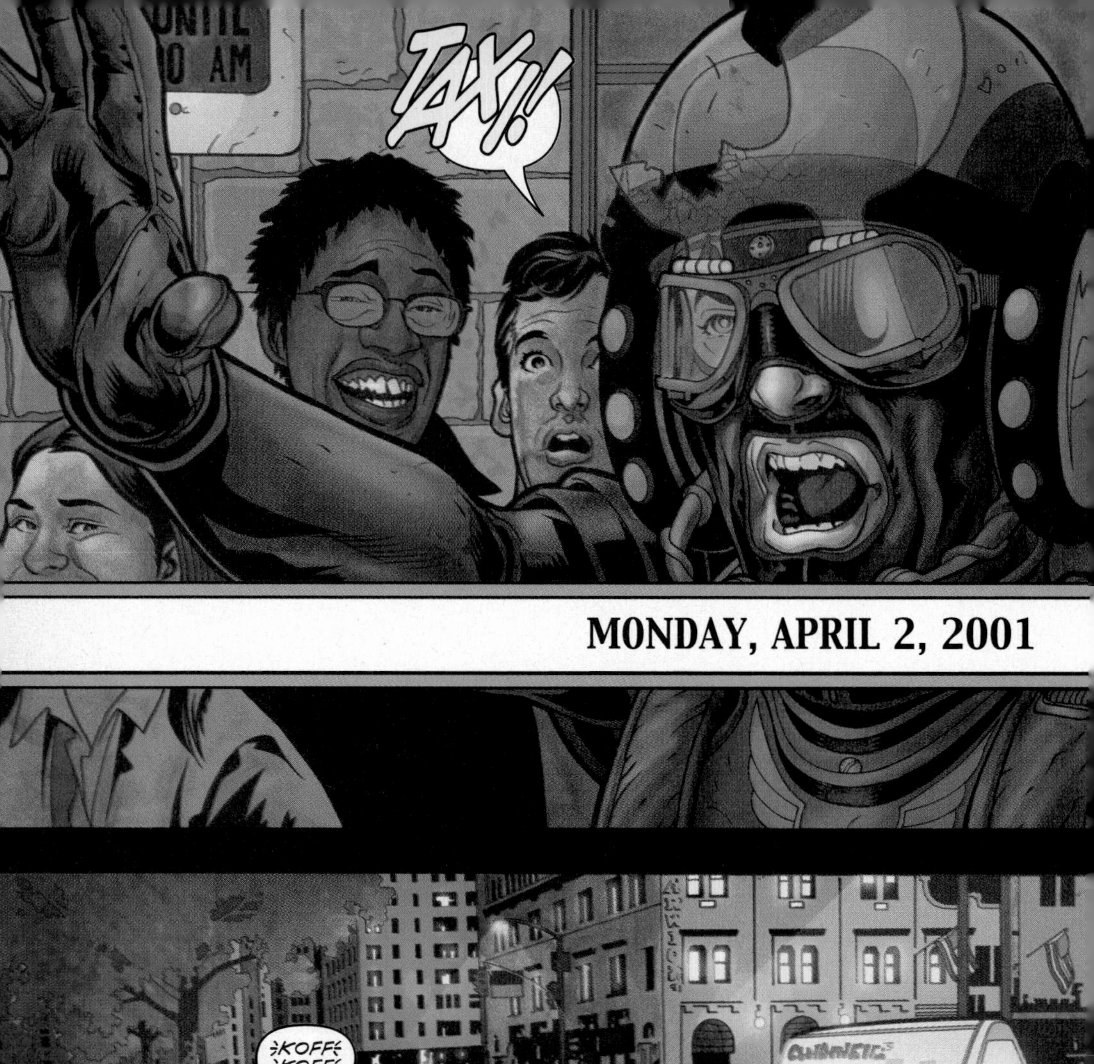
TAXI!!
MONDAY, APRIL 2, 2001

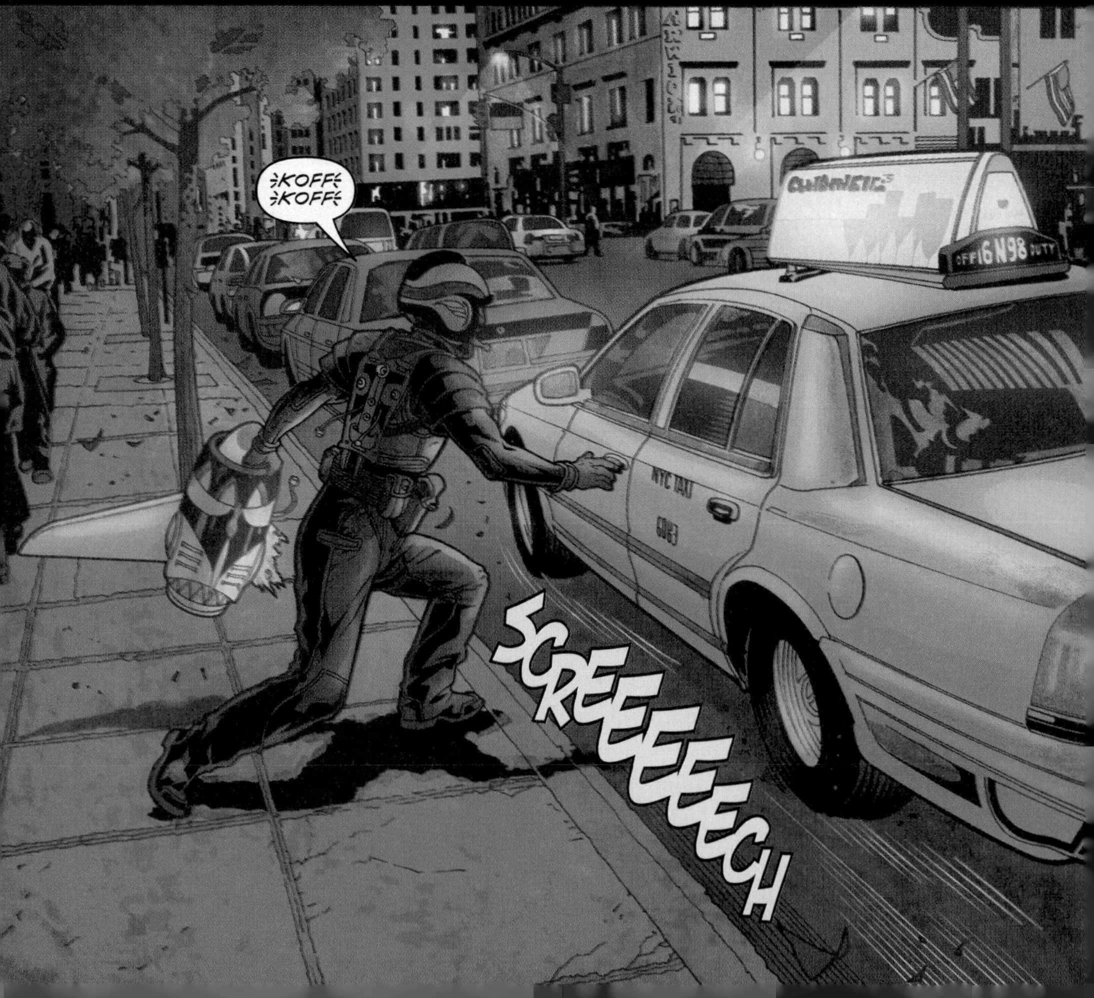
KOFF KOFF
SCREEEEEEECH

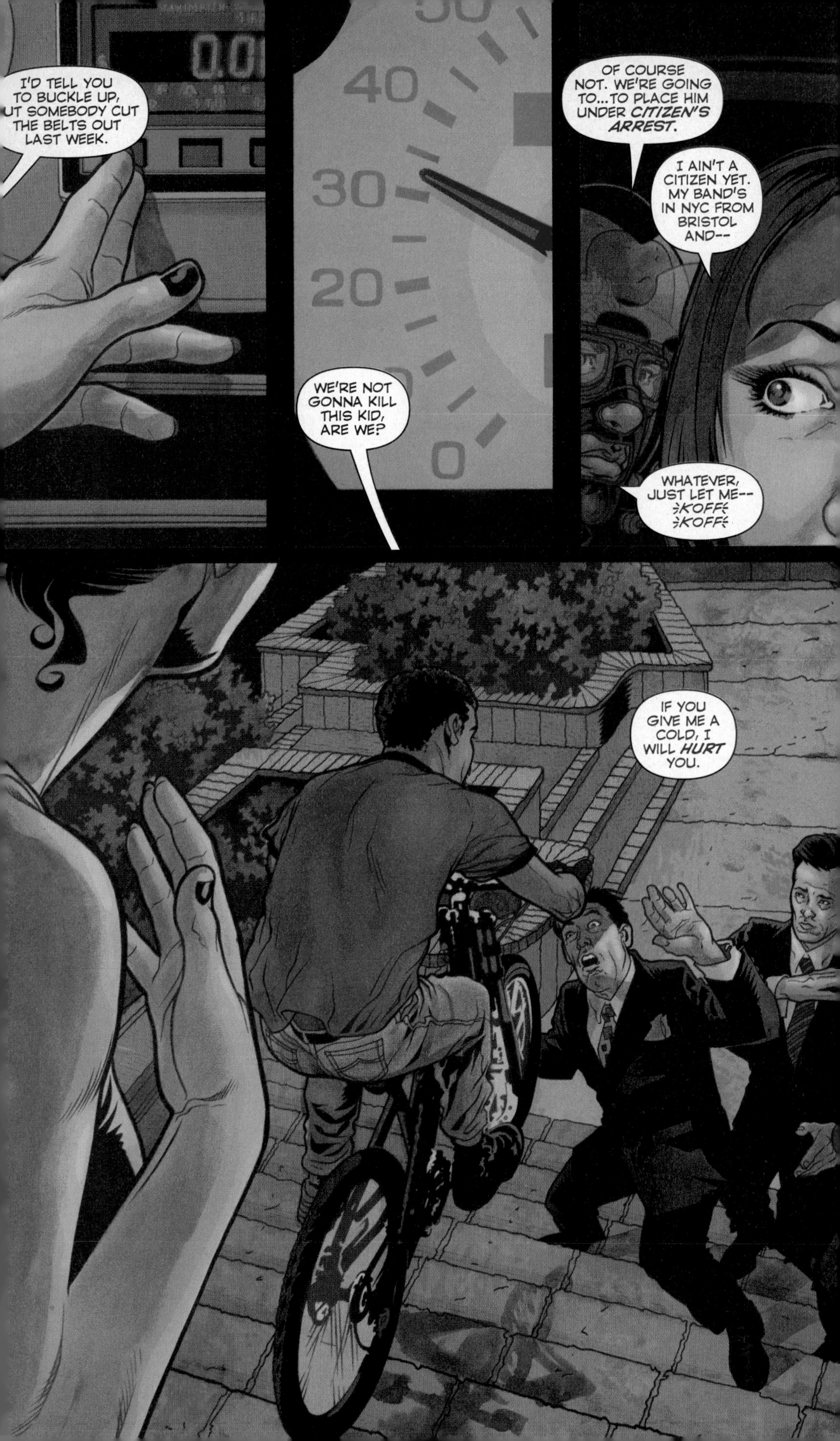
I'D TELL YOU TO BUCKLE UP, BUT SOMEBODY CUT THE BELTS OUT LAST WEEK.
WE'RE NOT GONNA KILL THIS KID, ARE WE?
OF COURSE NOT. WE'RE GOING TO...TO PLACE HIM UNDER *CITIZEN'S ARREST*.
I AIN'T A CITIZEN YET. MY BAND'S IN NYC FROM BRISTOL AND--
WHATEVER, JUST LET ME-- *KOFF* *KOFF*
IF YOU GIVE ME A COLD, I WILL *HURT* YOU.

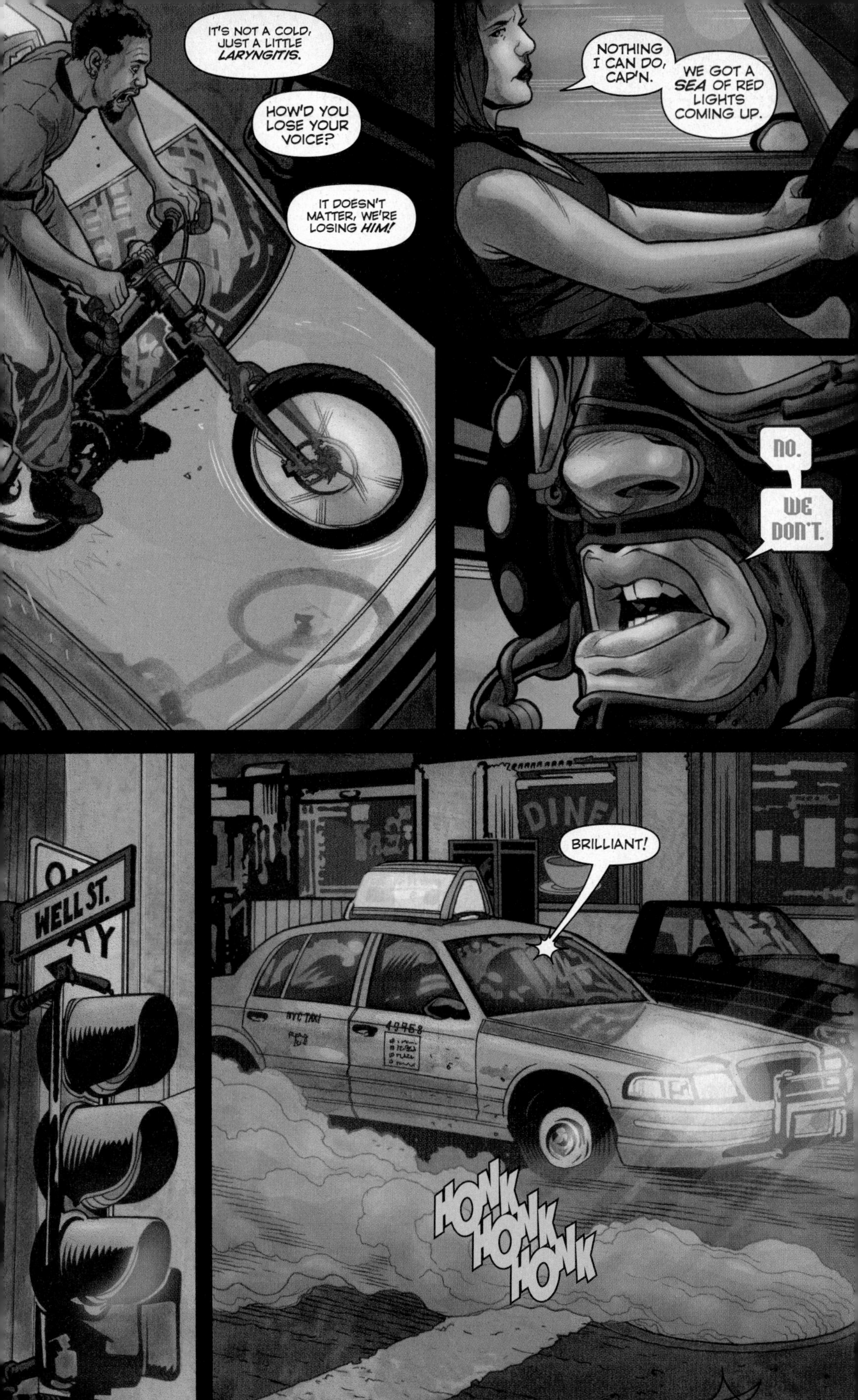
IT'S NOT A COLD, JUST A LITTLE LARYNGITIS.
HOW'D YOU LOSE YOUR VOICE?
IT DOESN'T MATTER, WE'RE LOSING HIM!
NOTHING I CAN DO, CAP'N.
WE GOT A SEA OF RED LIGHTS COMING UP.
NO.
WE DON'T.
WELL ST.
BRILLIANT!
NYC TAXI
HONK HONK HONK

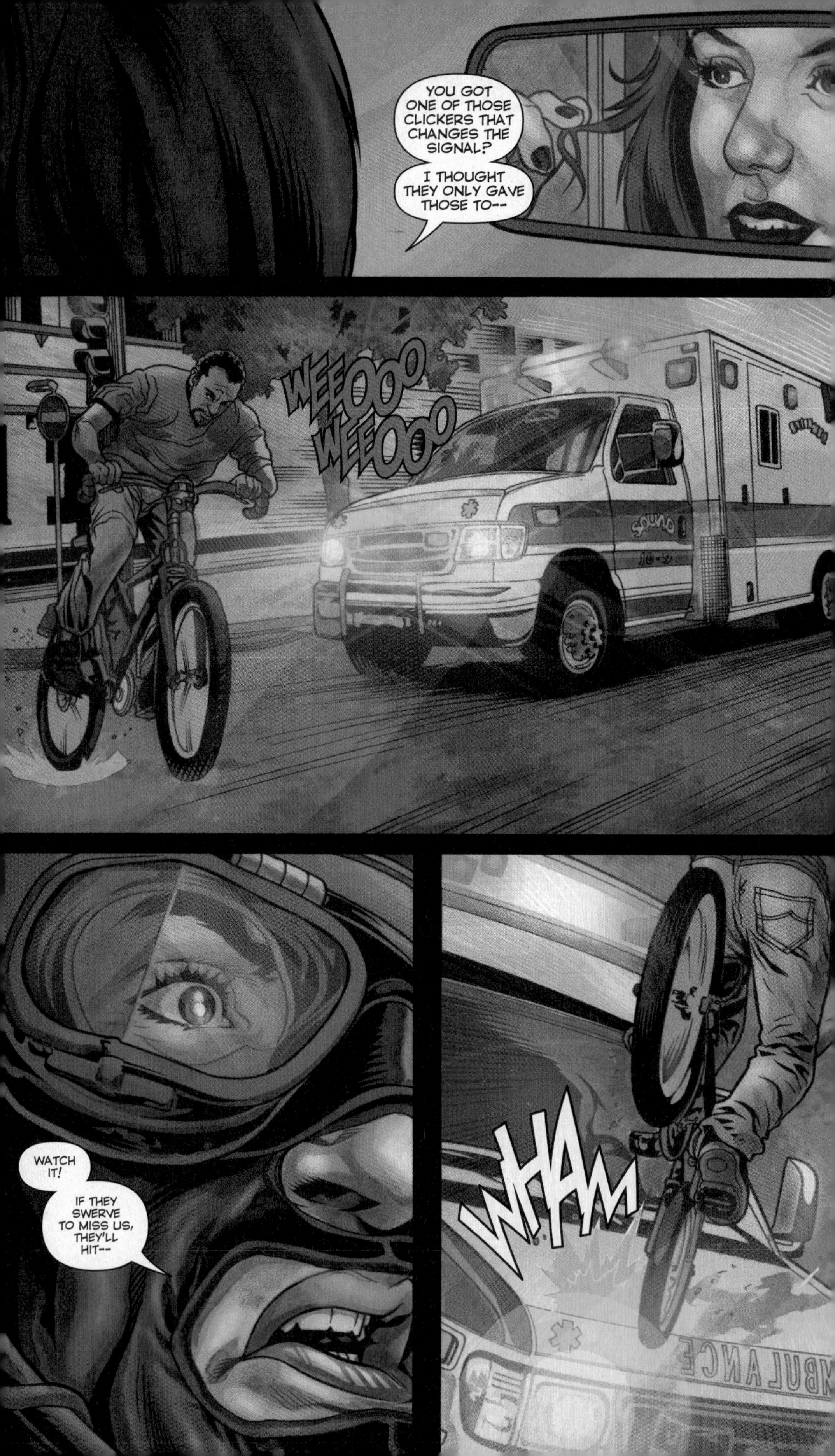
YOU GOT ONE OF THOSE CLICKERS THAT CHANGES THE SIGNAL?
I THOUGHT THEY ONLY GAVE THOSE TO--
WEEOOO WEEOOO
WATCH IT!
IF THEY SWERVE TO MISS US, THEY'LL HIT--
WHAM
AMBULANCE

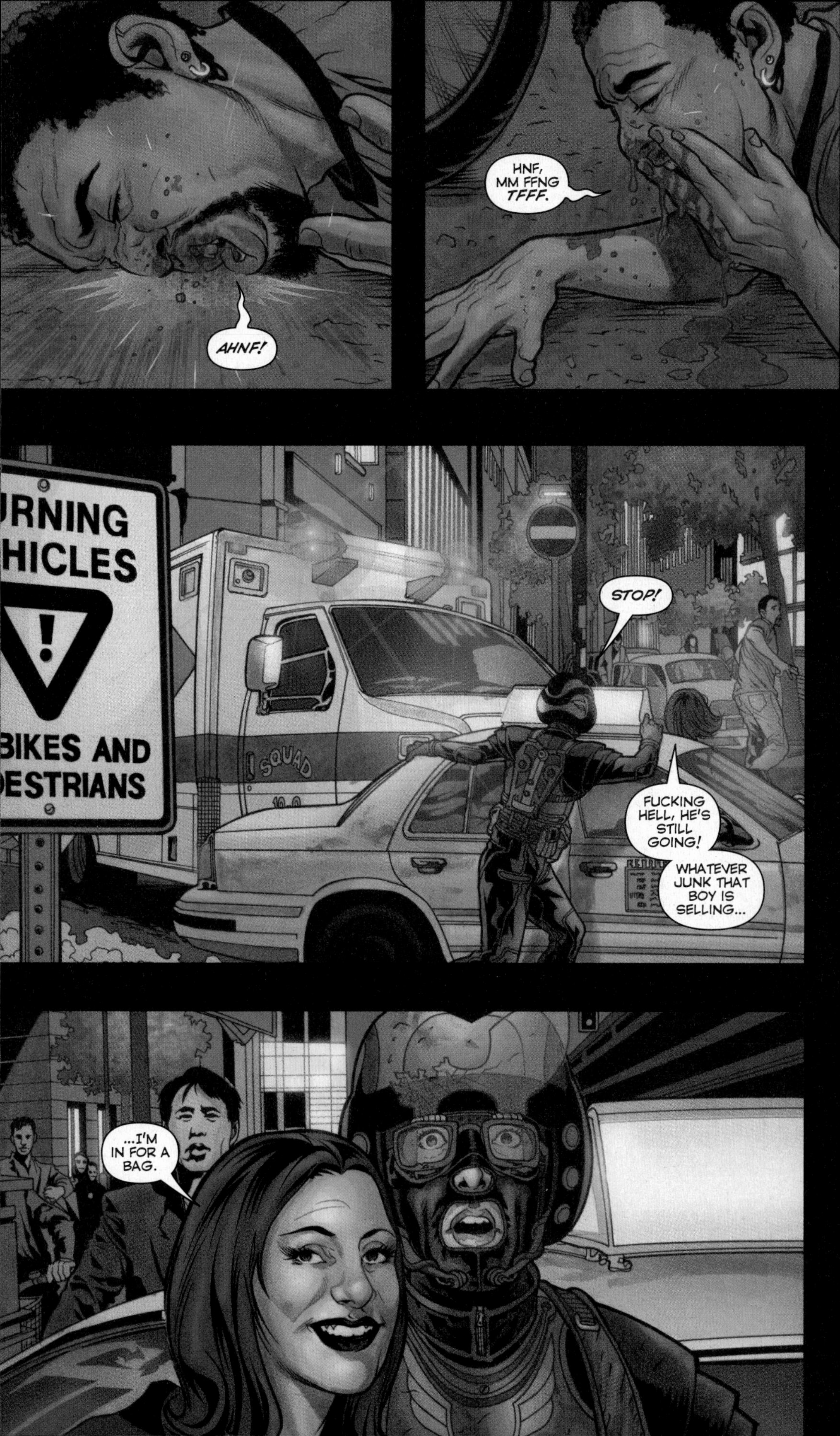
AHNF!
HNF, MM FFNG TFFF.
URNING
HICLES
!
BIKES AND
DESTRIANS
SQUAD
STOP!
FUCKING HELL, HE'S STILL GOING!
WHATEVER JUNK THAT BOY IS SELLING...
...I'M IN FOR A BAG.

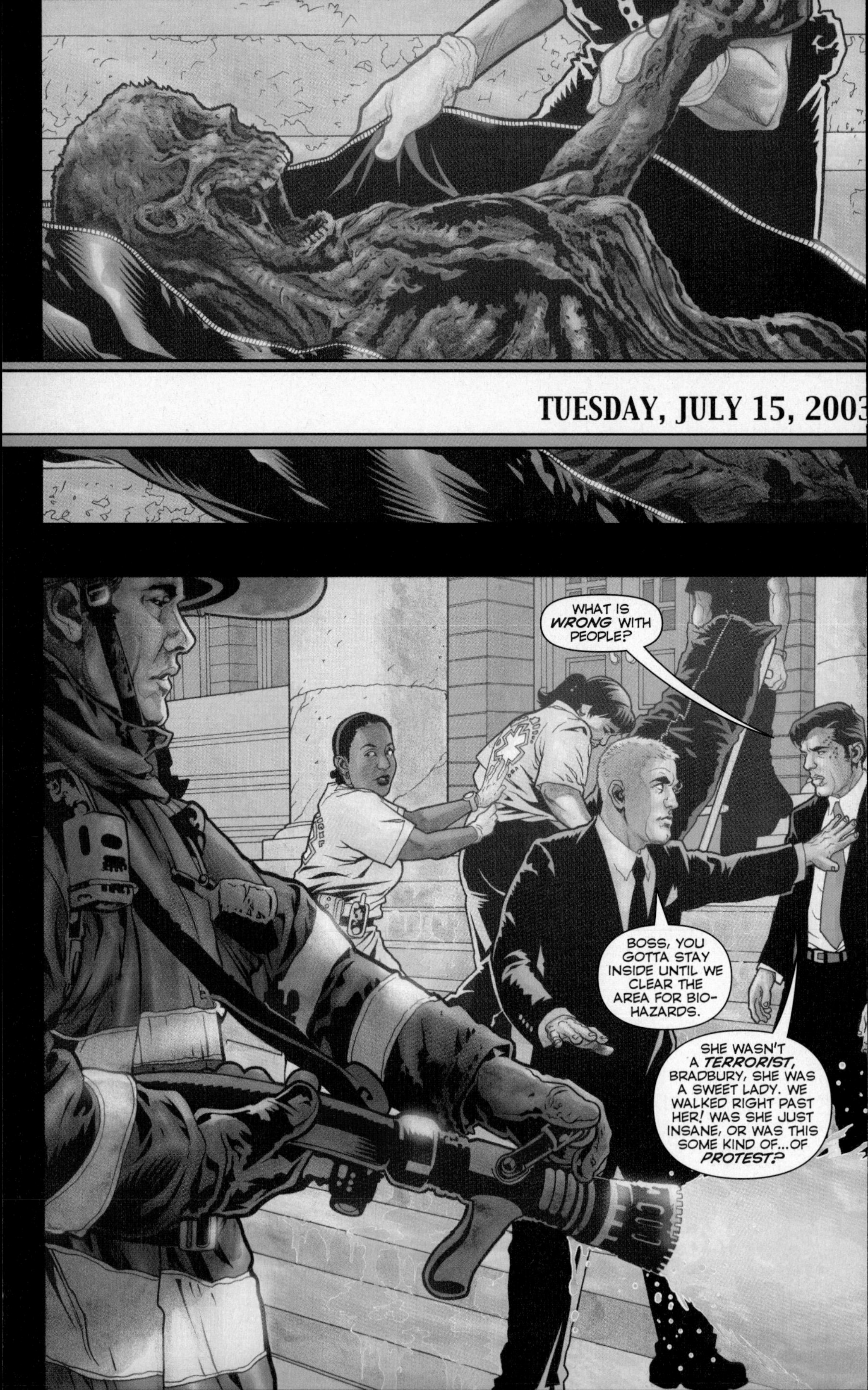
TUESDAY, JULY 15, 2003
WHAT IS *WRONG* WITH PEOPLE?
BOSS, YOU GOTTA STAY INSIDE UNTIL WE CLEAR THE AREA FOR BIO-HAZARDS.
SHE WASN'T A *TERRORIST,* BRADBURY, SHE WAS A SWEET LADY. WE WALKED RIGHT PAST HER! WAS SHE JUST INSANE, OR WAS THIS SOME KIND OF...OF *PROTEST?*

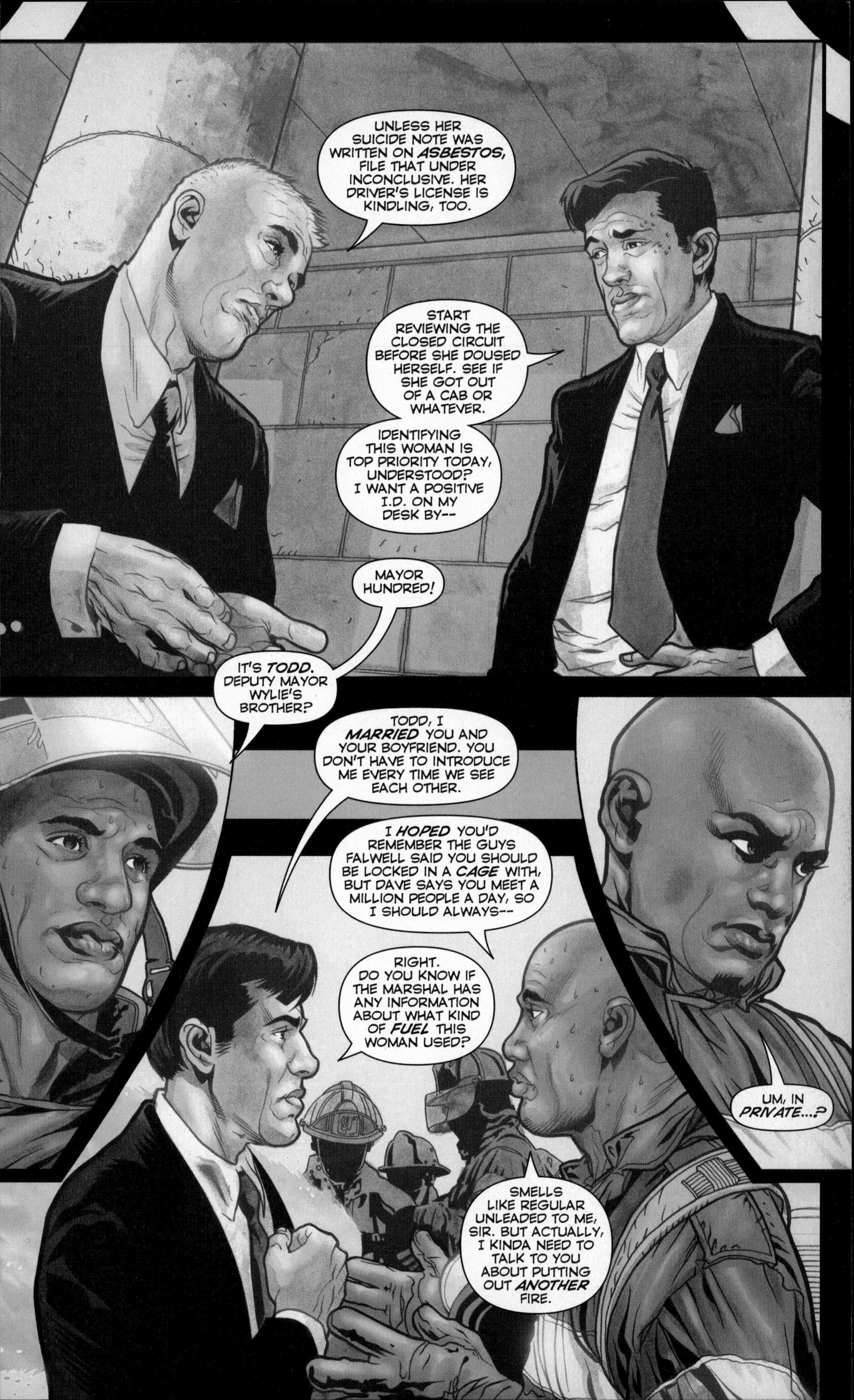
UNLESS HER SUICIDE NOTE WAS WRITTEN ON *ASBESTOS,* FILE THAT UNDER INCONCLUSIVE. HER DRIVER'S LICENSE IS KINDLING, TOO.
START REVIEWING THE CLOSED CIRCUIT BEFORE SHE DOUSED HERSELF. SEE IF SHE GOT OUT OF A CAB OR WHATEVER.
IDENTIFYING THIS WOMAN IS TOP PRIORITY TODAY, UNDERSTOOD? I WANT A POSITIVE I.D. ON MY DESK BY--
MAYOR HUNDRED!
IT'S *TODD.* DEPUTY MAYOR WYLIE'S BROTHER?
TODD, I *MARRIED* YOU AND YOUR BOYFRIEND. YOU DON'T HAVE TO INTRODUCE ME EVERY TIME WE SEE EACH OTHER.
I *HOPED* YOU'D REMEMBER THE GUYS FALWELL SAID YOU SHOULD BE LOCKED IN A *CAGE* WITH, BUT DAVE SAYS YOU MEET A MILLION PEOPLE A DAY, SO I SHOULD ALWAYS--
RIGHT. DO YOU KNOW IF THE MARSHAL HAS ANY INFORMATION ABOUT WHAT KIND OF *FUEL* THIS WOMAN USED?
UM, IN *PRIVATE...?*
SMELLS LIKE REGULAR UNLEADED TO ME, SIR. BUT ACTUALLY, I KINDA NEED TO TALK TO YOU ABOUT PUTTING OUT *ANOTHER* FIRE.

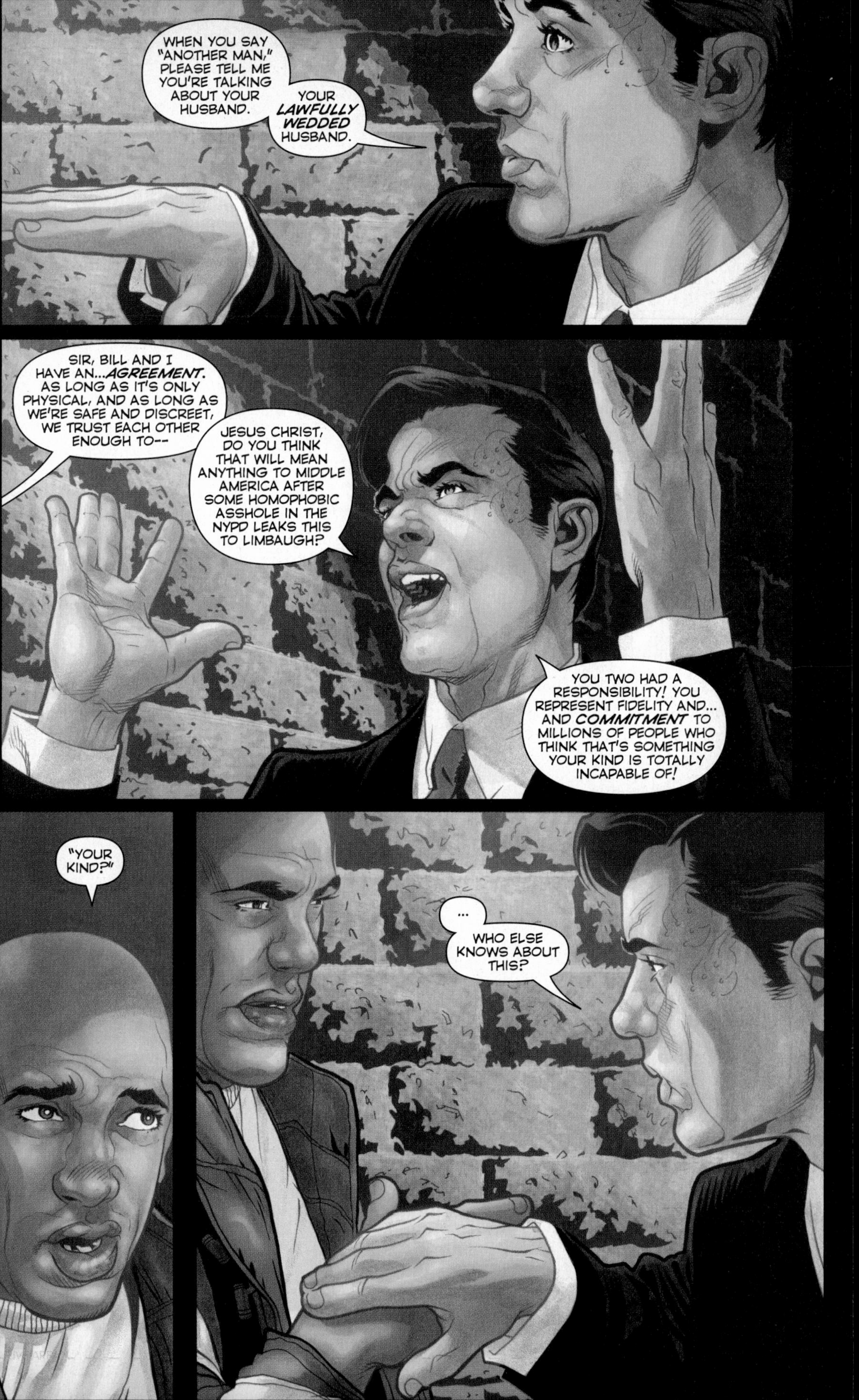
WHEN YOU SAY "ANOTHER MAN," PLEASE TELL ME YOU'RE TALKING ABOUT YOUR HUSBAND.
YOUR LAWFULLY WEDDED HUSBAND.
SIR, BILL AND I HAVE AN...AGREEMENT. AS LONG AS IT'S ONLY PHYSICAL, AND AS LONG AS WE'RE SAFE AND DISCREET, WE TRUST EACH OTHER ENOUGH TO--
JESUS CHRIST, DO YOU THINK THAT WILL MEAN ANYTHING TO MIDDLE AMERICA AFTER SOME HOMOPHOBIC ASSHOLE IN THE NYPD LEAKS THIS TO LIMBAUGH?
YOU TWO HAD A RESPONSIBILITY! YOU REPRESENT FIDELITY AND... AND COMMITMENT TO MILLIONS OF PEOPLE WHO THINK THAT'S SOMETHING YOUR KIND IS TOTALLY INCAPABLE OF!
"YOUR KIND?"
... WHO ELSE KNOWS ABOUT THIS?

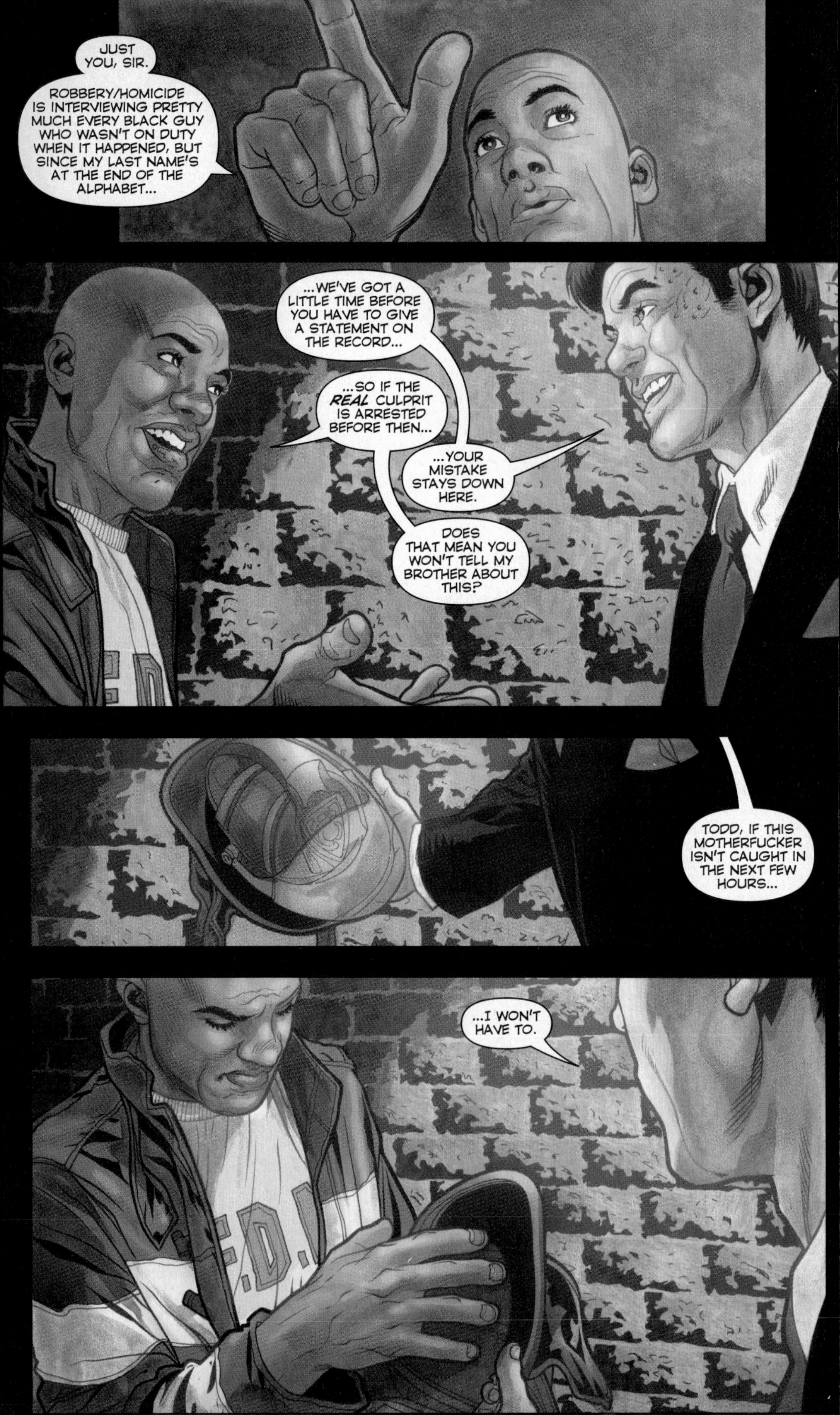

JUST YOU, SIR.
ROBBERY/HOMICIDE IS INTERVIEWING PRETTY MUCH EVERY BLACK GUY WHO WASN'T ON DUTY WHEN IT HAPPENED, BUT SINCE MY LAST NAME'S AT THE END OF THE ALPHABET...
...WE'VE GOT A LITTLE TIME BEFORE YOU HAVE TO GIVE A STATEMENT ON THE RECORD...
...SO IF THE REAL CULPRIT IS ARRESTED BEFORE THEN...
...YOUR MISTAKE STAYS DOWN HERE.
DOES THAT MEAN YOU WON'T TELL MY BROTHER ABOUT THIS?
TODD, IF THIS MOTHERFUCKER ISN'T CAUGHT IN THE NEXT FEW HOURS...
...I WON'T HAVE TO.

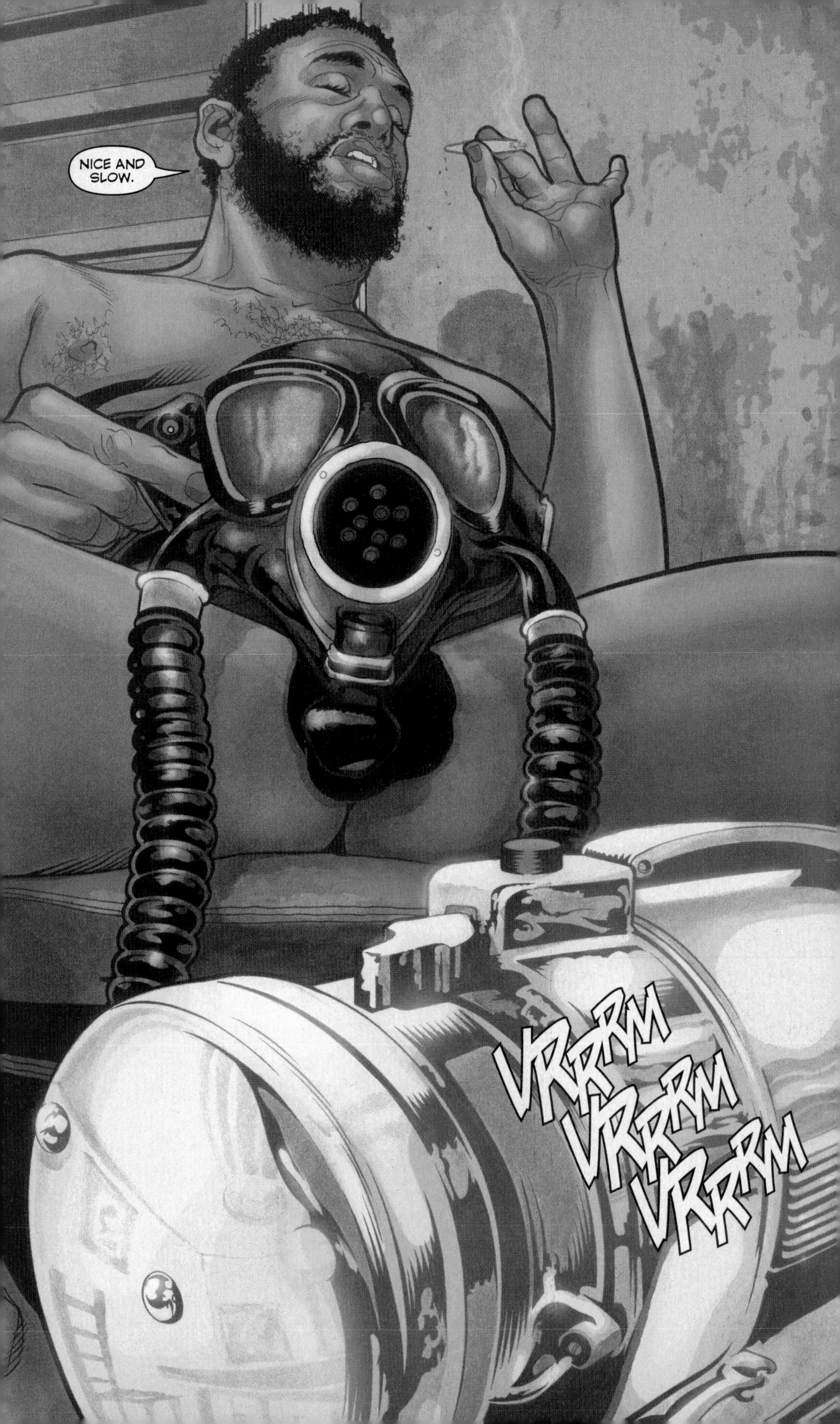
NICE AND SLOW.
VRRRM
VRRRM
VRRRM

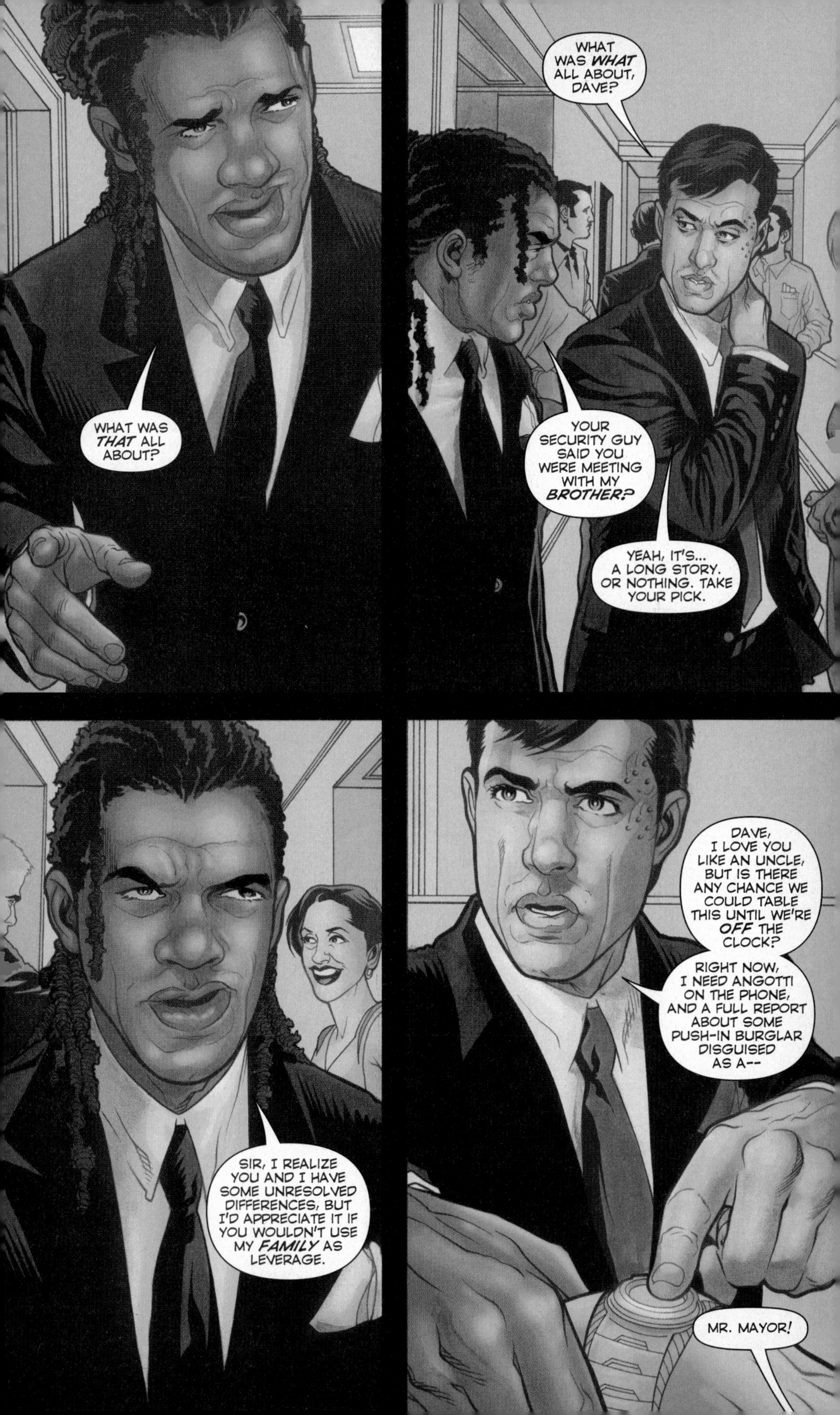
WHAT WAS *THAT* ALL ABOUT?
WHAT WAS *WHAT* ALL ABOUT, DAVE?
YOUR SECURITY GUY SAID YOU WERE MEETING WITH MY *BROTHER?*
YEAH, IT'S... A LONG STORY. OR NOTHING. TAKE YOUR PICK.
SIR, I REALIZE YOU AND I HAVE SOME UNRESOLVED DIFFERENCES, BUT I'D APPRECIATE IT IF YOU WOULDN'T USE MY *FAMILY* AS LEVERAGE.
DAVE, I LOVE YOU LIKE AN UNCLE, BUT IS THERE ANY CHANCE WE COULD TABLE THIS UNTIL WE'RE *OFF* THE CLOCK?
RIGHT NOW, I NEED ANGOTTI ON THE PHONE, AND A FULL REPORT ABOUT SOME PUSH-IN BURGLAR DISGUISED AS A--
MR. MAYOR!

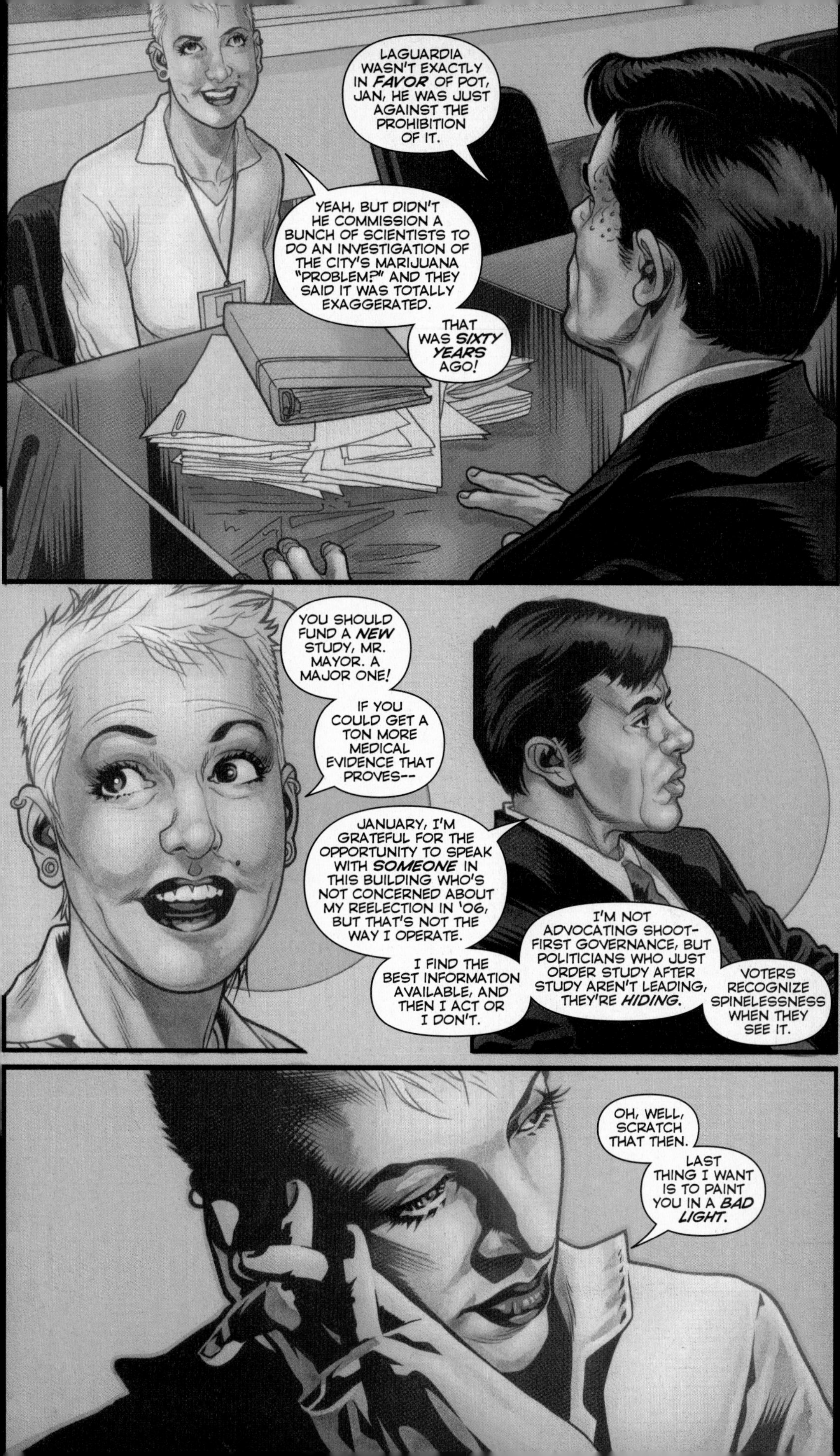
LAGUARDIA WASN'T EXACTLY IN FAVOR OF POT, JAN, HE WAS JUST AGAINST THE PROHIBITION OF IT.
YEAH, BUT DIDN'T HE COMMISSION A BUNCH OF SCIENTISTS TO DO AN INVESTIGATION OF THE CITY'S MARIJUANA "PROBLEM?" AND THEY SAID IT WAS TOTALLY EXAGGERATED.
THAT WAS SIXTY YEARS AGO!
YOU SHOULD FUND A NEW STUDY, MR. MAYOR. A MAJOR ONE!
IF YOU COULD GET A TON MORE MEDICAL EVIDENCE THAT PROVES--
JANUARY, I'M GRATEFUL FOR THE OPPORTUNITY TO SPEAK WITH SOMEONE IN THIS BUILDING WHO'S NOT CONCERNED ABOUT MY REELECTION IN '06, BUT THAT'S NOT THE WAY I OPERATE.
I FIND THE BEST INFORMATION AVAILABLE, AND THEN I ACT OR I DON'T.
I'M NOT ADVOCATING SHOOT-FIRST GOVERNANCE, BUT POLITICIANS WHO JUST ORDER STUDY AFTER STUDY AREN'T LEADING, THEY'RE HIDING.
VOTERS RECOGNIZE SPINELESSNESS WHEN THEY SEE IT.
OH, WELL, SCRATCH THAT THEN.
LAST THING I WANT IS TO PAINT YOU IN A BAD LIGHT.

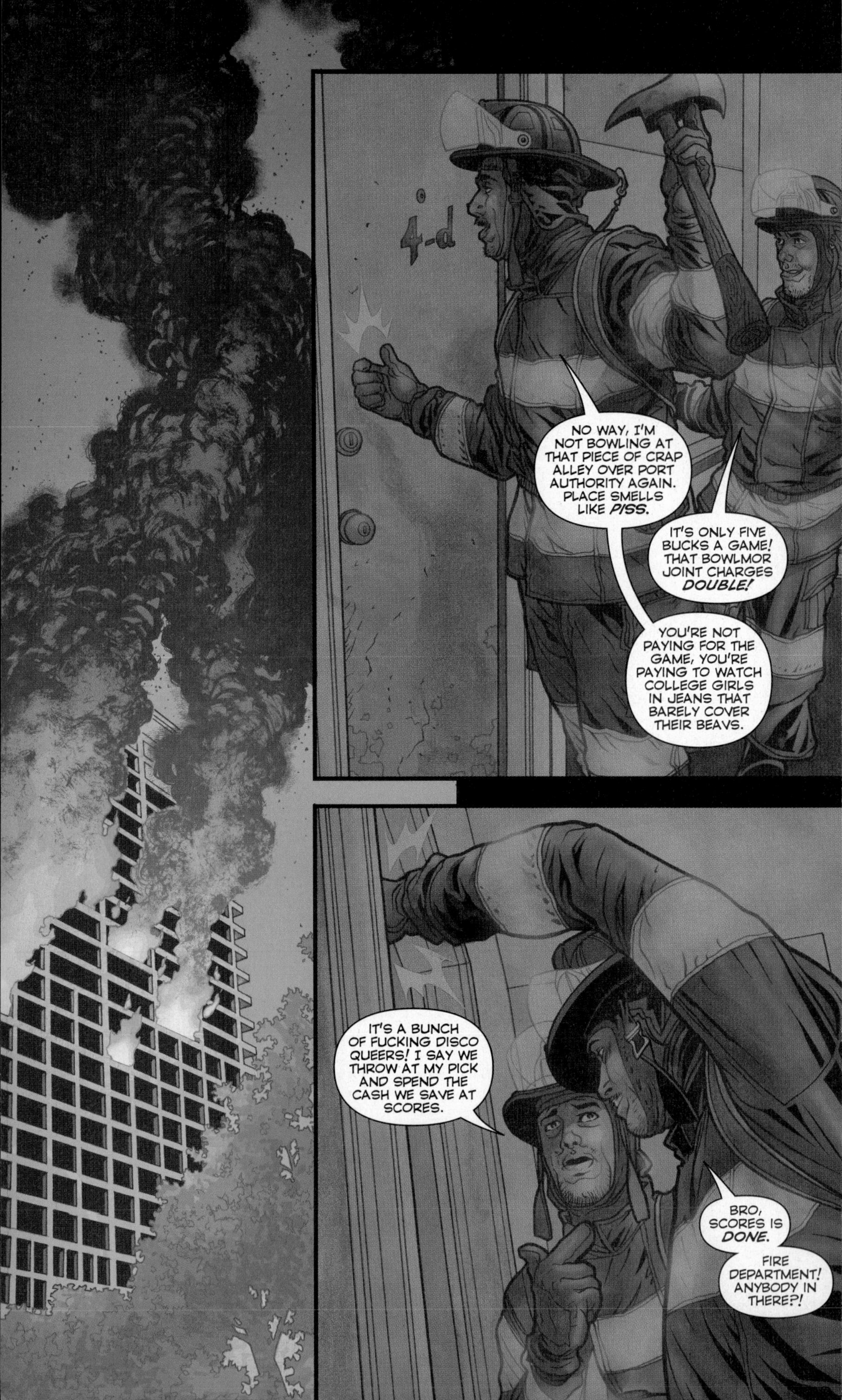
4-d
NO WAY, I'M NOT BOWLING AT THAT PIECE OF CRAP ALLEY OVER PORT AUTHORITY AGAIN. PLACE SMELLS LIKE *PISS*.
IT'S ONLY FIVE BUCKS A GAME! THAT BOWLMOR JOINT CHARGES *DOUBLE!*
YOU'RE NOT PAYING FOR THE GAME, YOU'RE PAYING TO WATCH COLLEGE GIRLS IN JEANS THAT BARELY COVER THEIR BEAVS.
IT'S A BUNCH OF FUCKING DISCO QUEERS! I SAY WE THROW AT MY PICK AND SPEND THE CASH WE SAVE AT SCORES.
BRO, SCORES IS *DONE*.
FIRE DEPARTMENT! ANYBODY IN THERE?!

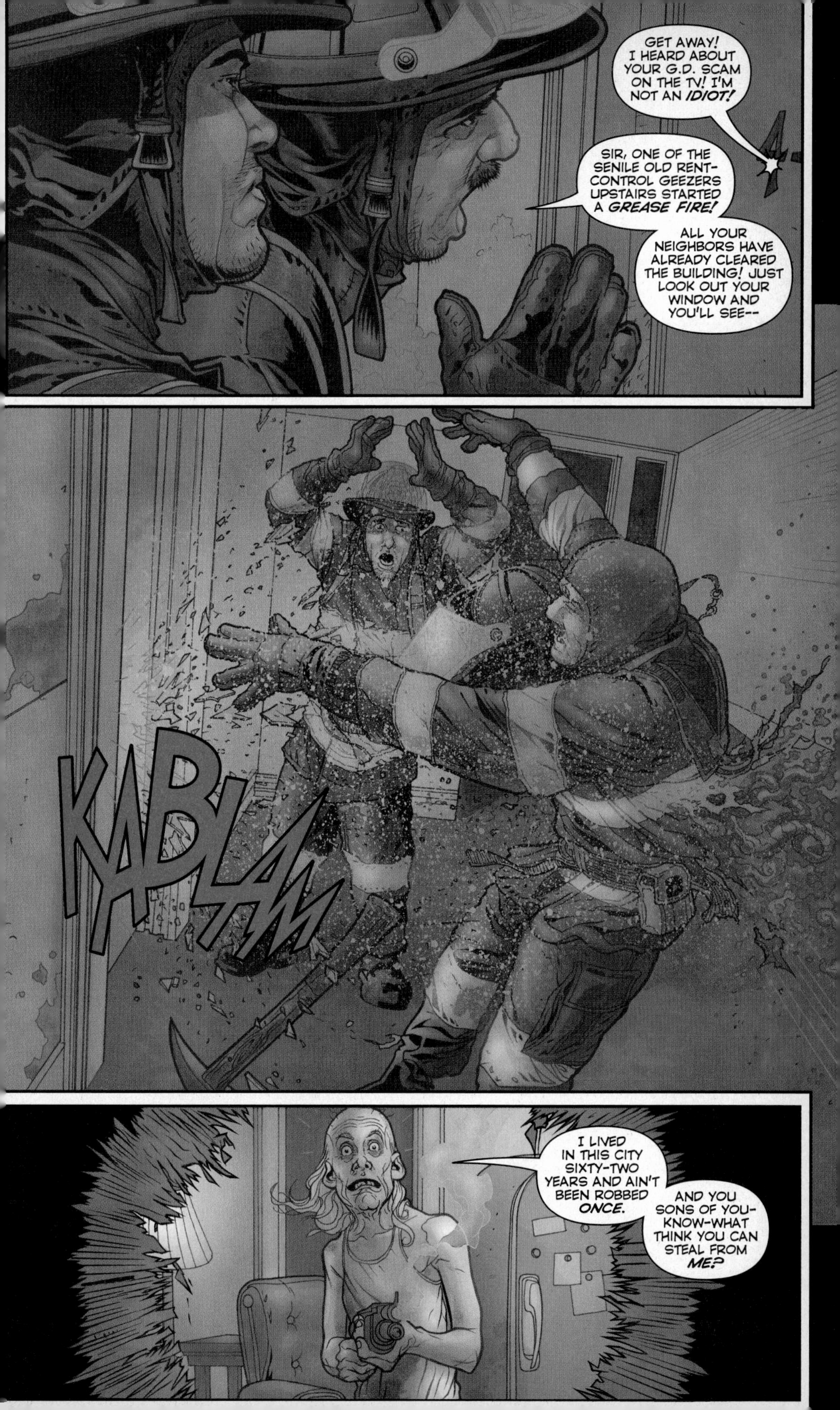
GET AWAY! I HEARD ABOUT YOUR G.D. SCAM ON THE TV! I'M NOT AN *IDIOT!*
SIR, ONE OF THE SENILE OLD RENT-CONTROL GEEZERS UPSTAIRS STARTED A *GREASE FIRE!*
ALL YOUR NEIGHBORS HAVE ALREADY CLEARED THE BUILDING! JUST LOOK OUT YOUR WINDOW AND YOU'LL SEE--
KABLAM
I LIVED IN THIS CITY SIXTY-TWO YEARS AND AIN'T BEEN ROBBED *ONCE*.
AND YOU SONS OF YOU-KNOW-WHAT THINK YOU CAN STEAL FROM *ME?*

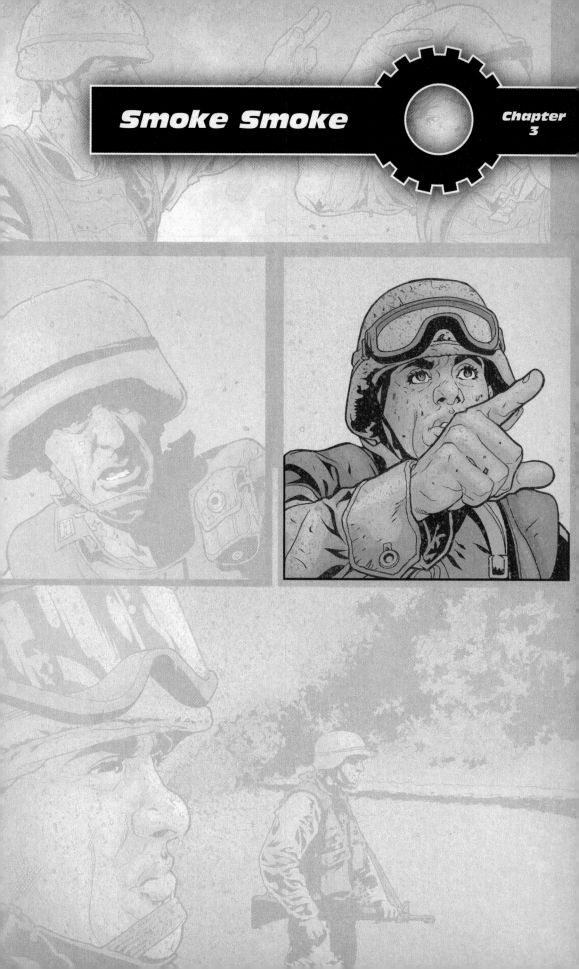

Smoke Smoke

Chapter 3

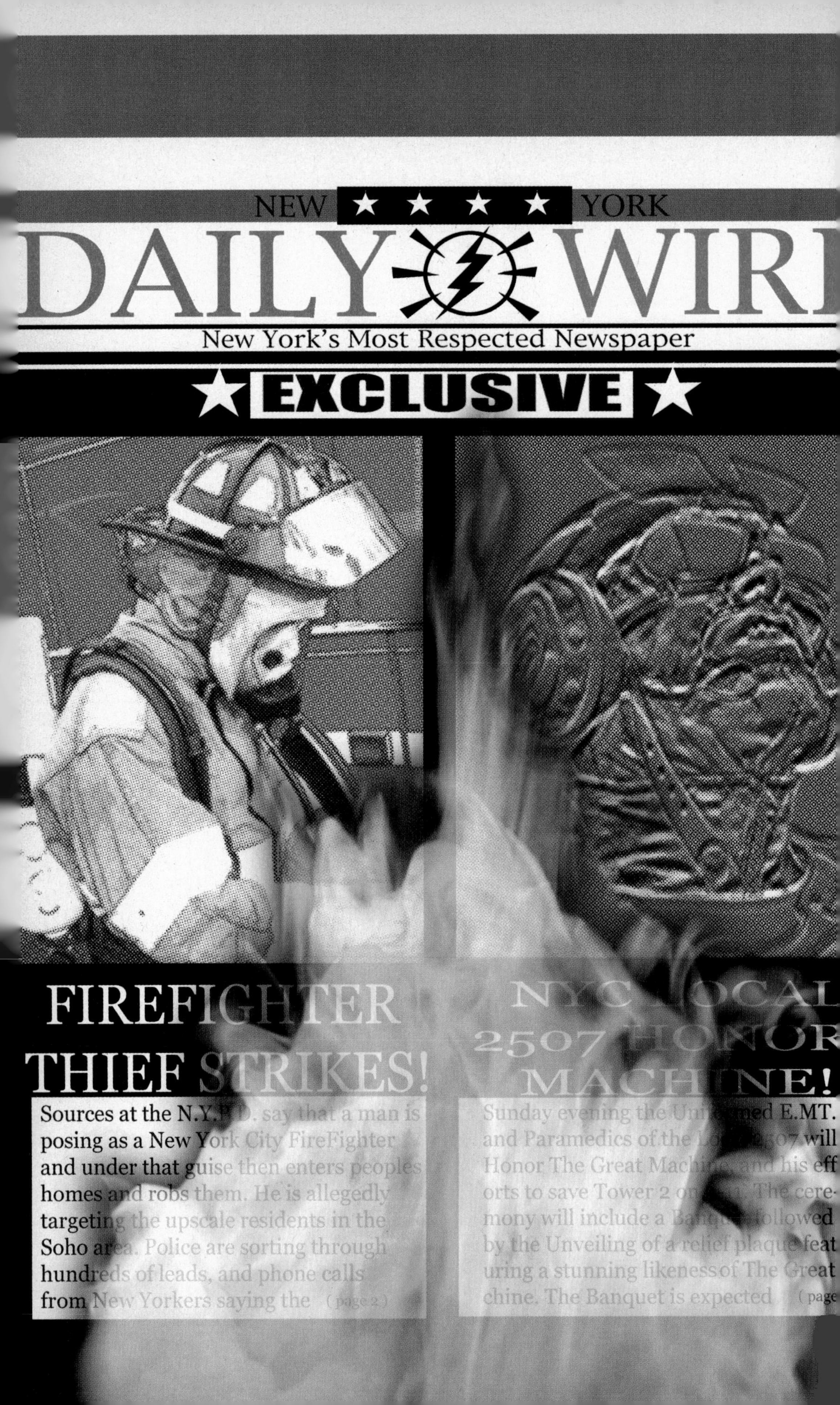

NEW ★ ★ ★ ★ YORK
DAILY ⚡ WIRE

New York's Most Respected Newspaper

★ EXCLUSIVE ★

FIREFIGHTER THIEF STRIKES!

Sources at the N.Y.P.D. say that a man is posing as a New York City FireFighter and under that guise then enters peoples homes and robs them. He is allegedly targeting the upscale residents in the Soho area. Police are sorting through hundreds of leads, and phone calls from New Yorkers saying the (page 2)

NYC LOCAL 2507 HONOR MACHINE!

Sunday evening the Uniformed E.MT. and Paramedics of the Local 2507 will Honor The Great Machine and his efforts to save Tower 2 on 9/11. The ceremony will include a Banquet followed by the Unveiling of a relief plaque featuring a stunning likeness of The Great Machine. The Banquet is expected (page

MONDAY, APRIL 2, 2001

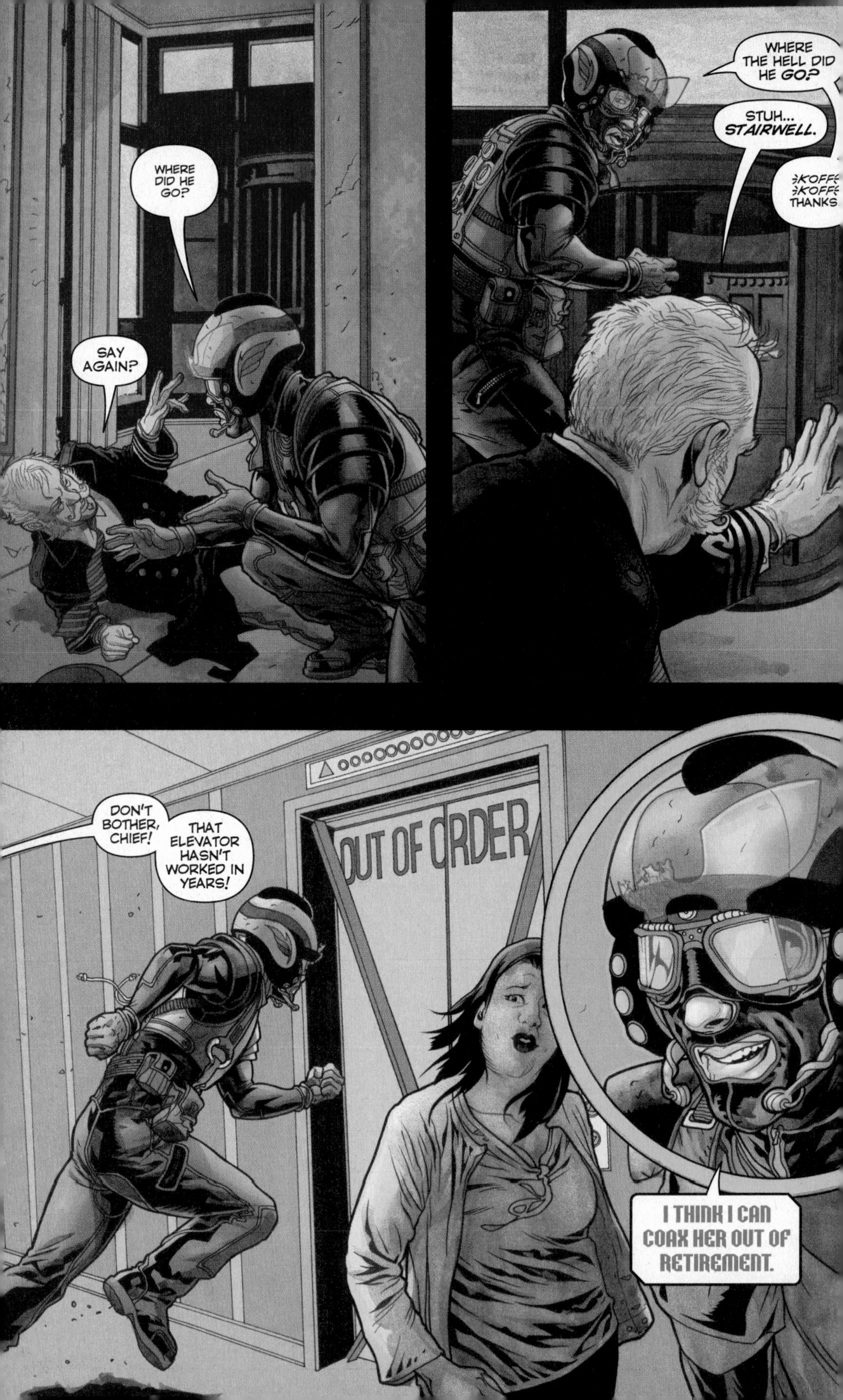
WHERE DID HE GO?
SAY AGAIN?
WHERE THE HELL DID HE GO?
STUH... STAIRWELL.
KOFF KOFF THANKS
DON'T BOTHER, CHIEF!
THAT ELEVATOR HASN'T WORKED IN YEARS!
OUT OF ORDER
I THINK I CAN COAX HER OUT OF RETIREMENT.

MITCHELL, LET HIM GO!

NO PUSHER BOY IS WORTH *DYING* FOR!

YOU STICK WITH A JOB UNTIL IT'S *FINISHED*, KREMLIN.

BUT BRADBURY SAYS THERE IS DELI GETTING *ROBBED* TWO BLOCK'S FROM YOU! THOSE PEOPLE NEED YOU MORE THAN--

CLEVELAND, DON'T!

YOU'LL NEVER MAKE IT!

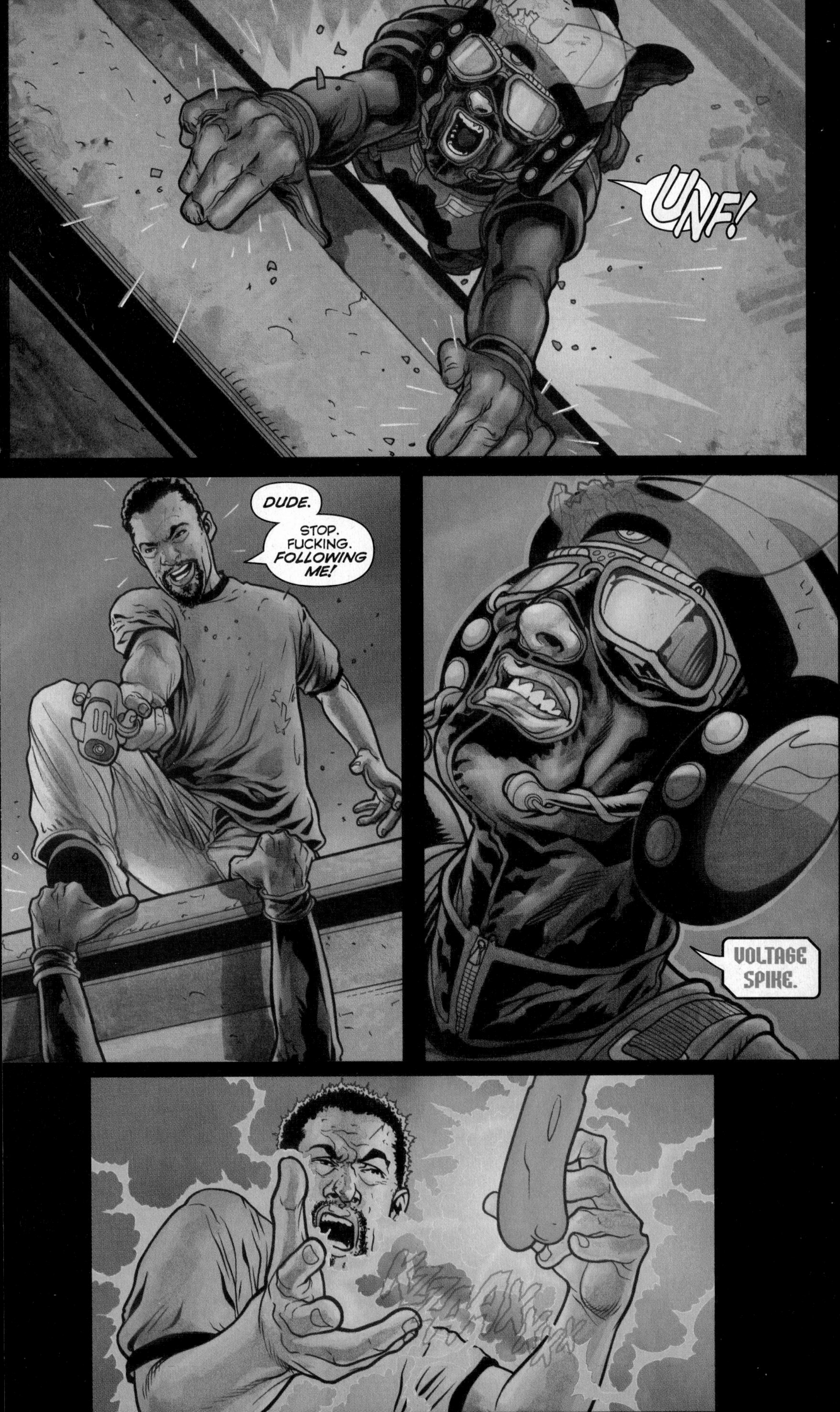
UNF!
DUDE.
STOP. FUCKING. FOLLOWING ME!
VOLTAGE SPIKE.

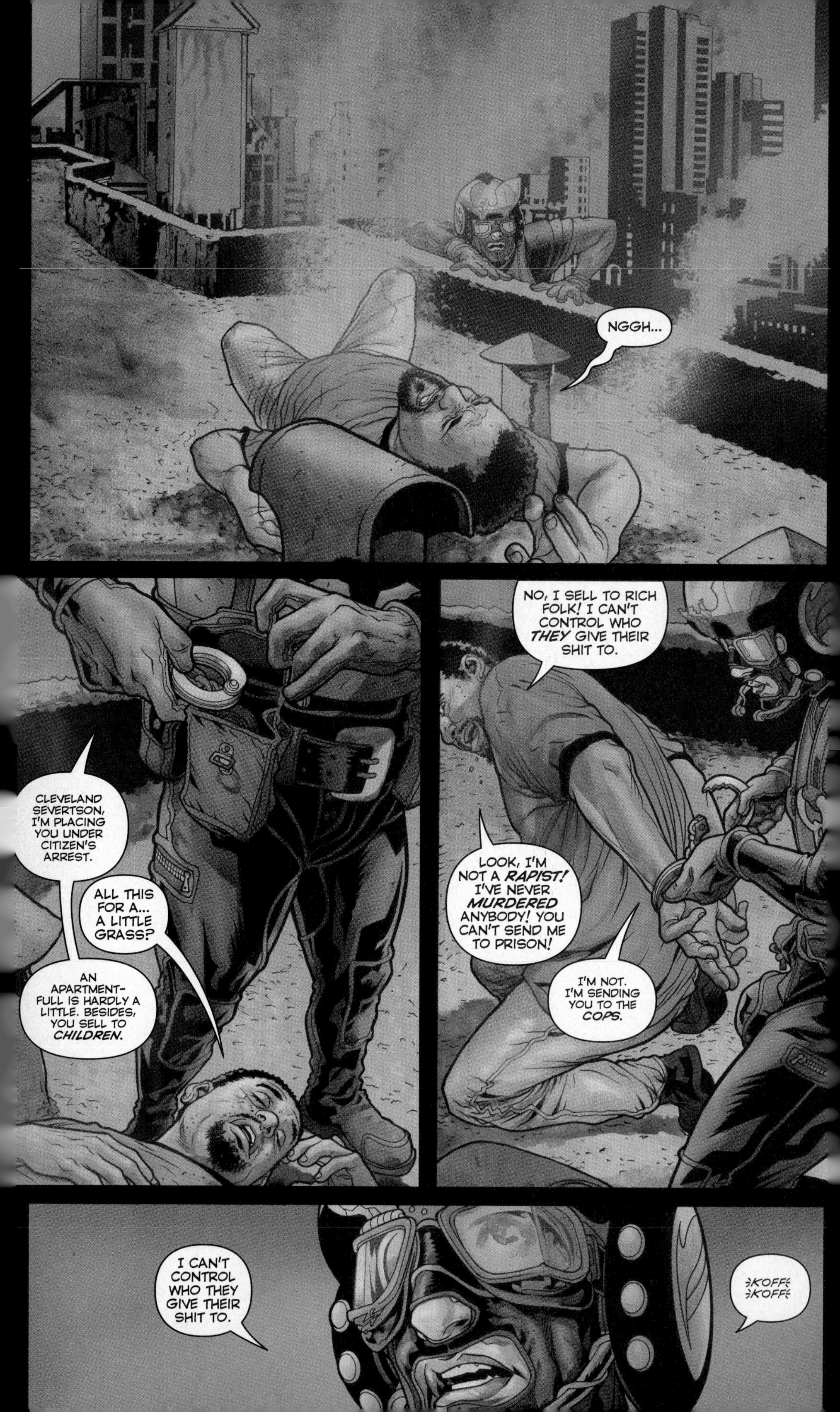
NGGH...
CLEVELAND SEVERTSON, I'M PLACING YOU UNDER CITIZEN'S ARREST.
ALL THIS FOR A... A LITTLE GRASS?
AN APARTMENT-FULL IS HARDLY A LITTLE. BESIDES, YOU SELL TO CHILDREN.
NO, I SELL TO RICH FOLK! I CAN'T CONTROL WHO THEY GIVE THEIR SHIT TO.
LOOK, I'M NOT A RAPIST! I'VE NEVER MURDERED ANYBODY! YOU CAN'T SEND ME TO PRISON!
I'M NOT. I'M SENDING YOU TO THE COPS.
I CAN'T CONTROL WHO THEY GIVE THEIR SHIT TO.
KOFF KOFF

TUESDAY, JULY 15, 2003

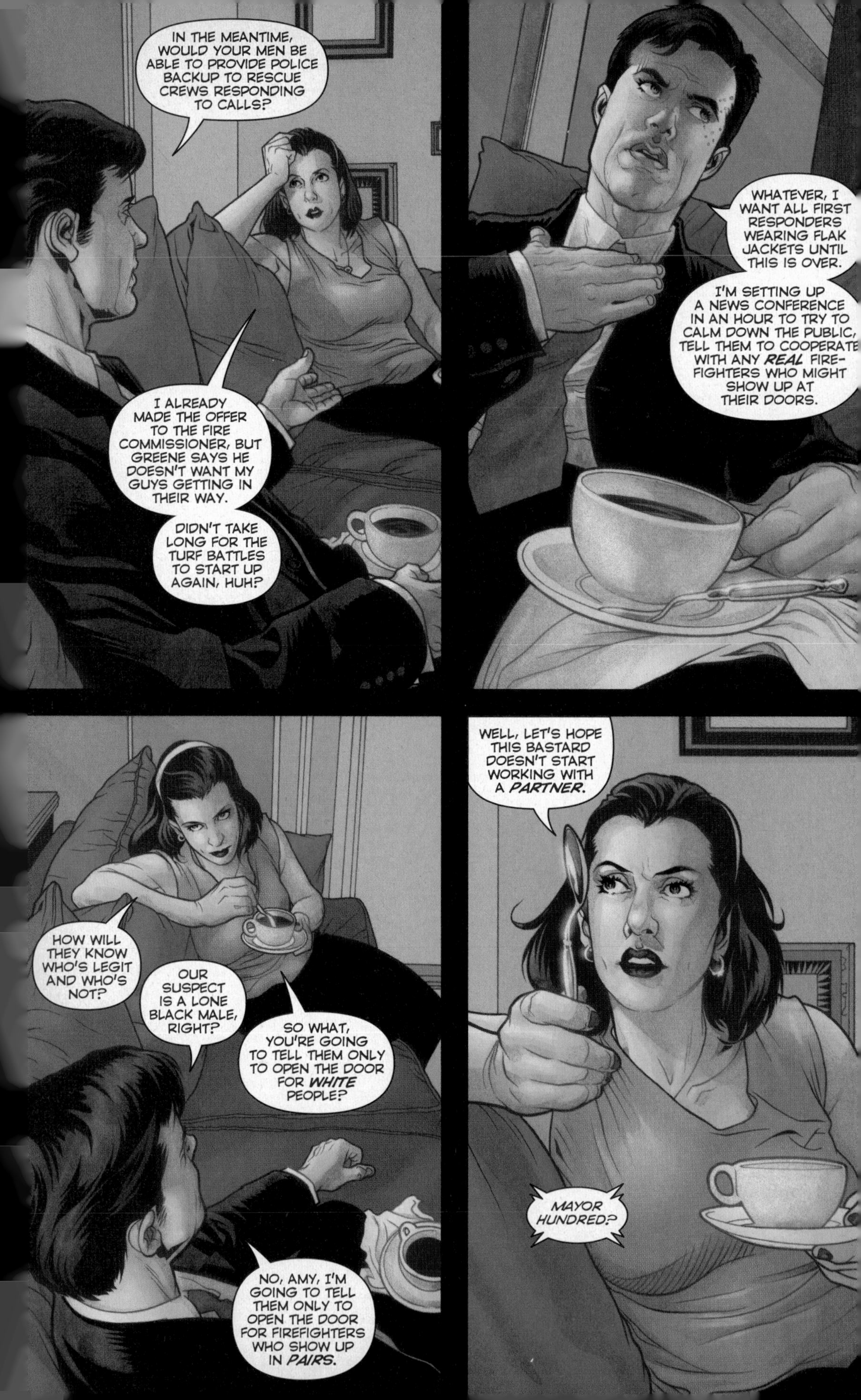
IN THE MEANTIME, WOULD YOUR MEN BE ABLE TO PROVIDE POLICE BACKUP TO RESCUE CREWS RESPONDING TO CALLS?
I ALREADY MADE THE OFFER TO THE FIRE COMMISSIONER, BUT GREENE SAYS HE DOESN'T WANT MY GUYS GETTING IN THEIR WAY.
DIDN'T TAKE LONG FOR THE TURF BATTLES TO START UP AGAIN, HUH?
WHATEVER, I WANT ALL FIRST RESPONDERS WEARING FLAK JACKETS UNTIL THIS IS OVER.
I'M SETTING UP A NEWS CONFERENCE IN AN HOUR TO TRY TO CALM DOWN THE PUBLIC, TELL THEM TO COOPERATE WITH ANY *REAL* FIRE-FIGHTERS WHO MIGHT SHOW UP AT THEIR DOORS.
HOW WILL THEY KNOW WHO'S LEGIT AND WHO'S NOT?
OUR SUSPECT IS A LONE BLACK MALE, RIGHT?
SO WHAT, YOU'RE GOING TO TELL THEM ONLY TO OPEN THE DOOR FOR *WHITE* PEOPLE?
NO, AMY, I'M GOING TO TELL THEM ONLY TO OPEN THE DOOR FOR FIREFIGHTERS WHO SHOW UP IN *PAIRS*.
WELL, LET'S HOPE THIS BASTARD DOESN'T START WORKING WITH A *PARTNER*.
MAYOR HUNDRED?

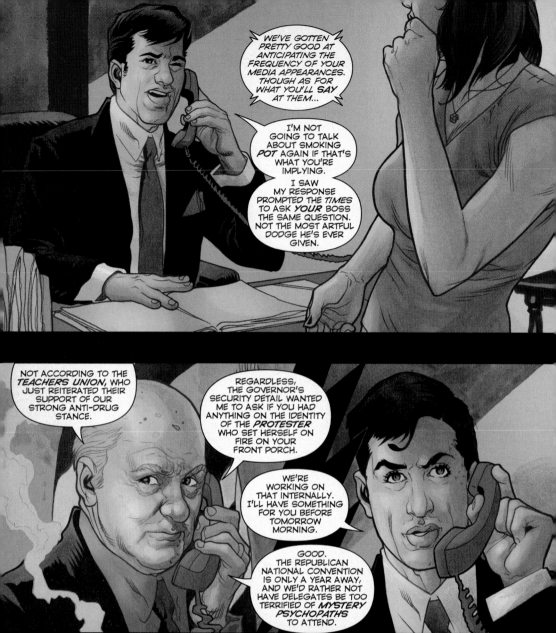

WE'VE GOTTEN PRETTY GOOD AT ANTICIPATING THE FREQUENCY OF YOUR MEDIA APPEARANCES. THOUGH AS FOR WHAT YOU'LL *SAY* AT THEM...

I'M NOT GOING TO TALK ABOUT SMOKING *POT* AGAIN IF THAT'S WHAT YOU'RE IMPLYING.

I SAW MY RESPONSE PROMPTED THE *TIMES* TO ASK *YOUR* BOSS THE SAME QUESTION. NOT THE MOST ARTFUL DODGE HE'S EVER GIVEN.

NOT ACCORDING TO THE *TEACHERS UNION,* WHO JUST REITERATED THEIR SUPPORT OF OUR STRONG ANTI-DRUG STANCE.

REGARDLESS, THE GOVERNOR'S SECURITY DETAIL WANTED ME TO ASK IF YOU HAD ANYTHING ON THE IDENTITY OF THE *PROTESTER* WHO SET HERSELF ON FIRE ON YOUR FRONT PORCH.

WE'RE WORKING ON THAT INTERNALLY. I'LL HAVE SOMETHING FOR YOU BEFORE TOMORROW MORNING.

GOOD. THE REPUBLICAN NATIONAL CONVENTION IS ONLY A YEAR AWAY, AND WE'D RATHER NOT HAVE DELEGATES BE TOO TERRIFIED OF *MYSTERY PSYCHOPATHS* TO ATTEND.

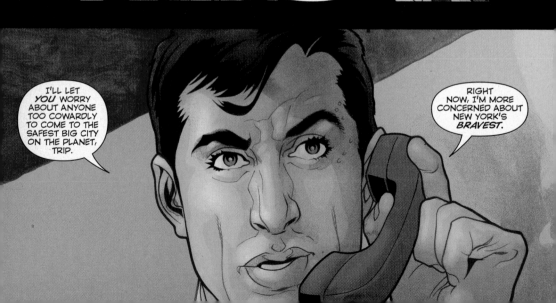

I'LL LET *YOU* WORRY ABOUT ANYONE TOO COWARDLY TO COME TO THE SAFEST BIG CITY ON THE PLANET, TRIP.

RIGHT NOW, I'M MORE CONCERNED ABOUT NEW YORK'S *BRAVEST.*

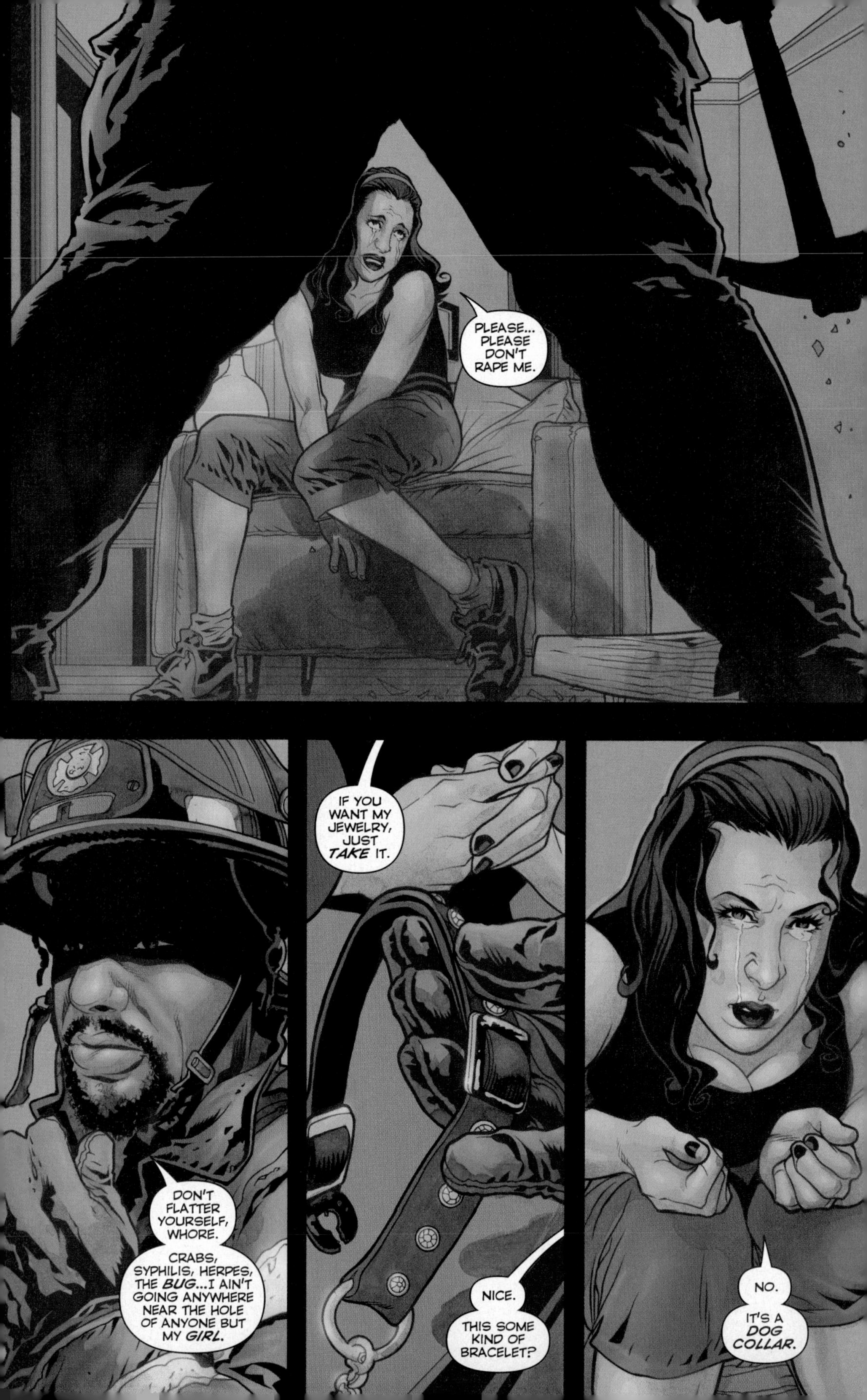
PLEASE... PLEASE DON'T RAPE ME.
DON'T FLATTER YOURSELF, WHORE.
CRABS, SYPHILIS, HERPES, THE BUG...I AIN'T GOING ANYWHERE NEAR THE HOLE OF ANYONE BUT MY GIRL.
IF YOU WANT MY JEWELRY, JUST TAKE IT.
NICE.
THIS SOME KIND OF BRACELET?
NO.
IT'S A DOG COLLAR.

ARK
ARK
ARK
ARK

KILL HIM! SWALLOW HIS FREAKING BALLS!

NAH!

GET IT OFF!

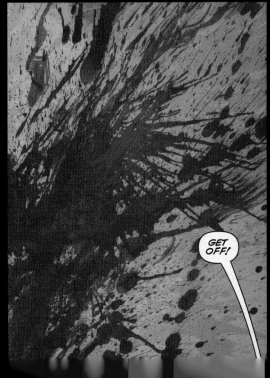

GET OFF!

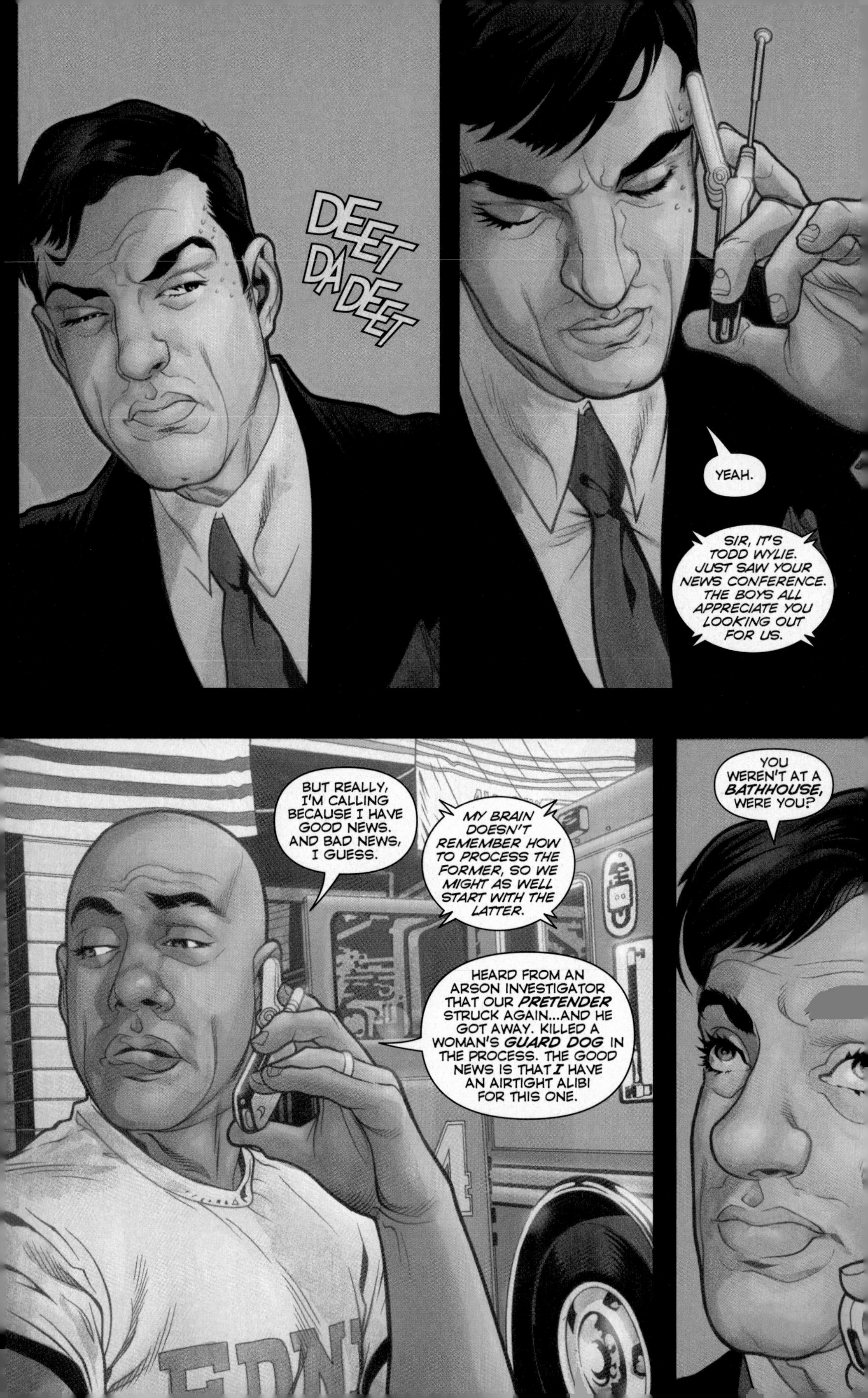
DEET DADEET
YEAH.
SIR, IT'S TODD WYLIE. JUST SAW YOUR NEWS CONFERENCE. THE BOYS ALL APPRECIATE YOU LOOKING OUT FOR US.
BUT REALLY, I'M CALLING BECAUSE I HAVE GOOD NEWS. AND BAD NEWS, I GUESS.
MY BRAIN DOESN'T REMEMBER HOW TO PROCESS THE FORMER, SO WE MIGHT AS WELL START WITH THE LATTER.
HEARD FROM AN ARSON INVESTIGATOR THAT OUR PRETENDER STRUCK AGAIN...AND HE GOT AWAY. KILLED A WOMAN'S GUARD DOG IN THE PROCESS. THE GOOD NEWS IS THAT I HAVE AN AIRTIGHT ALIBI FOR THIS ONE.
YOU WEREN'T AT A BATHHOUSE, WERE YOU?

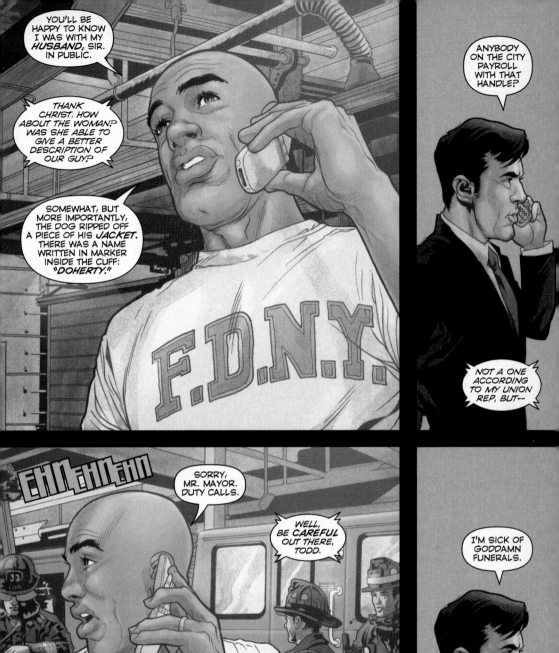

YOU'LL BE HAPPY TO KNOW I WAS WITH MY *HUSBAND*, SIR. IN PUBLIC.

THANK *CHRIST*. HOW ABOUT THE WOMAN? WAS SHE ABLE TO GIVE A BETTER DESCRIPTION OF OUR GUY?

SOMEWHAT, BUT MORE IMPORTANTLY, THE DOG RIPPED OFF A PIECE OF HIS *JACKET*. THERE WAS A NAME WRITTEN IN MARKER INSIDE THE CUFF: *"DOHERTY."*

ANYBODY ON THE CITY PAYROLL WITH THAT HANDLE?

NOT A ONE ACCORDING TO MY UNION REP, BUT--

EHN EHN EHN

SORRY, MR. MAYOR. DUTY CALLS.

WELL, BE *CAREFUL* OUT THERE, TODD.

I'M SICK OF GODDAMN FUNERALS.

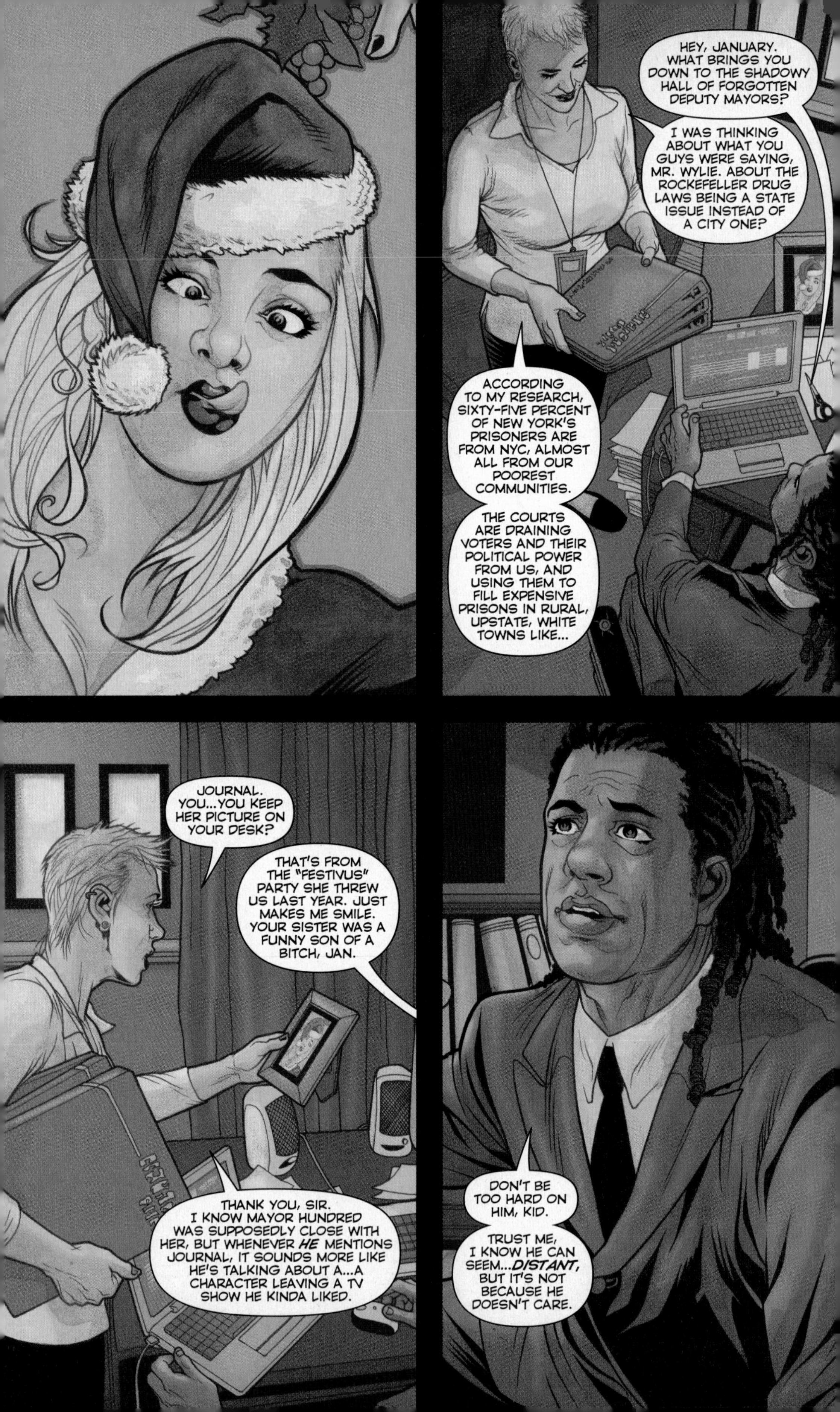
HEY, JANUARY. WHAT BRINGS YOU DOWN TO THE SHADOWY HALL OF FORGOTTEN DEPUTY MAYORS?
I WAS THINKING ABOUT WHAT YOU GUYS WERE SAYING, MR. WYLIE. ABOUT THE ROCKEFELLER DRUG LAWS BEING A STATE ISSUE INSTEAD OF A CITY ONE?
ACCORDING TO MY RESEARCH, SIXTY-FIVE PERCENT OF NEW YORK'S PRISONERS ARE FROM NYC, ALMOST ALL FROM OUR POOREST COMMUNITIES.
THE COURTS ARE DRAINING VOTERS AND THEIR POLITICAL POWER FROM US, AND USING THEM TO FILL EXPENSIVE PRISONS IN RURAL, UPSTATE, WHITE TOWNS LIKE...
JOURNAL. YOU...YOU KEEP HER PICTURE ON YOUR DESK?
THAT'S FROM THE "FESTIVUS" PARTY SHE THREW US LAST YEAR. JUST MAKES ME SMILE. YOUR SISTER WAS A FUNNY SON OF A BITCH, JAN.
THANK YOU, SIR. I KNOW MAYOR HUNDRED WAS SUPPOSEDLY CLOSE WITH HER, BUT WHENEVER *HE* MENTIONS JOURNAL, IT SOUNDS MORE LIKE HE'S TALKING ABOUT A...A CHARACTER LEAVING A TV SHOW HE KINDA LIKED.
DON'T BE TOO HARD ON HIM, KID.
TRUST ME, I KNOW HE CAN SEEM...*DISTANT*, BUT IT'S NOT BECAUSE HE DOESN'T CARE.

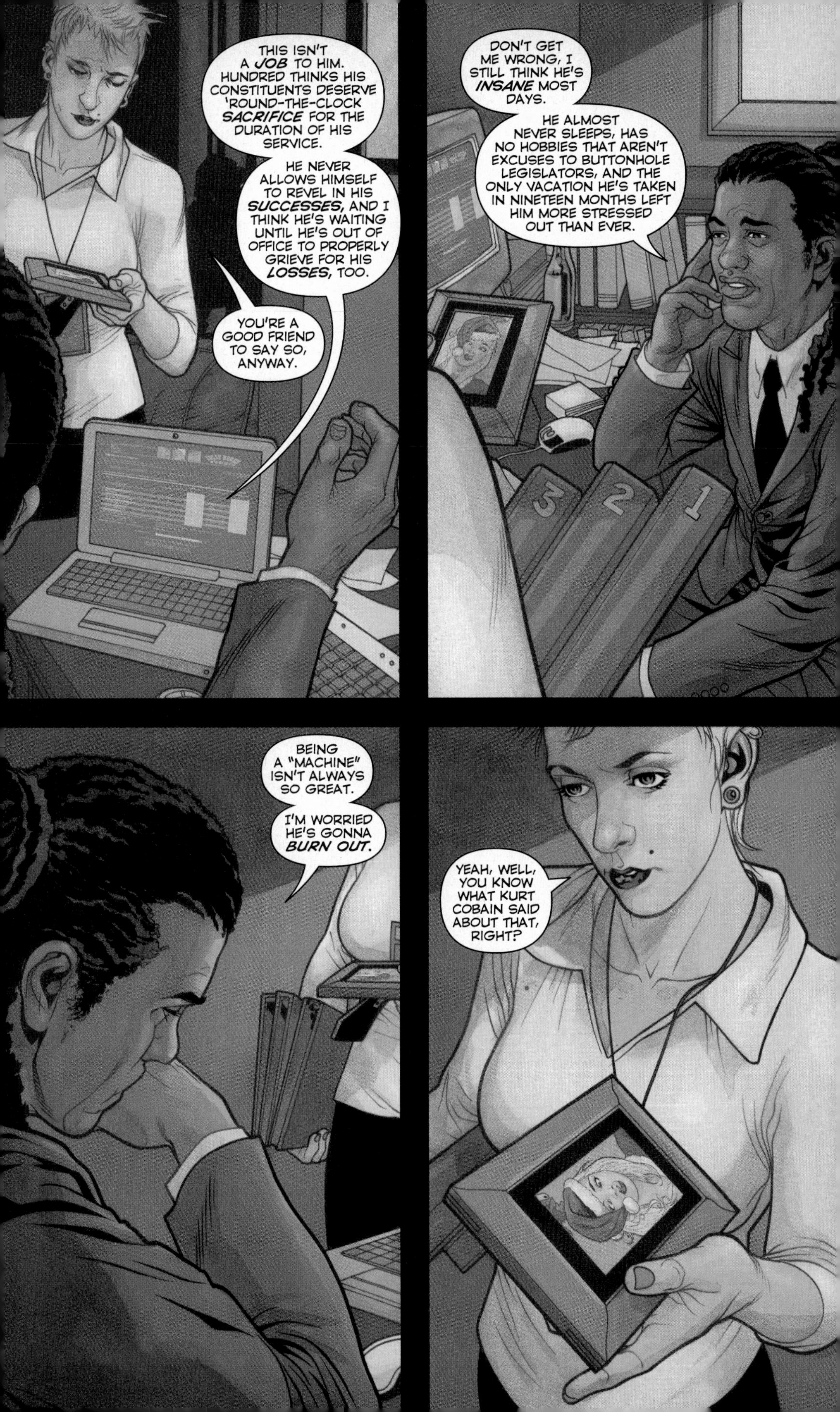
THIS ISN'T A JOB TO HIM. HUNDRED THINKS HIS CONSTITUENTS DESERVE 'ROUND-THE-CLOCK SACRIFICE FOR THE DURATION OF HIS SERVICE.
HE NEVER ALLOWS HIMSELF TO REVEL IN HIS SUCCESSES, AND I THINK HE'S WAITING UNTIL HE'S OUT OF OFFICE TO PROPERLY GRIEVE FOR HIS LOSSES, TOO.
YOU'RE A GOOD FRIEND TO SAY SO, ANYWAY.
DON'T GET ME WRONG, I STILL THINK HE'S INSANE MOST DAYS.
HE ALMOST NEVER SLEEPS, HAS NO HOBBIES THAT AREN'T EXCUSES TO BUTTONHOLE LEGISLATORS, AND THE ONLY VACATION HE'S TAKEN IN NINETEEN MONTHS LEFT HIM MORE STRESSED OUT THAN EVER.
3
2
1
BEING A "MACHINE" ISN'T ALWAYS SO GREAT.
I'M WORRIED HE'S GONNA BURN OUT.
YEAH, WELL, YOU KNOW WHAT KURT COBAIN SAID ABOUT THAT, RIGHT?

DO ME A FAVOR, BRADBURY. WHEN YOU WANT US TO RENDEZVOUS AT OUR SECRET *"DEEPTHROAT SPOT,"* DON'T TEXT THOSE WORDS DIRECTLY TO MY EVER-SUSPICIOUS *SECRETARY.*

OOPS. SORRY, BOSS.

I JUST DON'T LIKE TALKING ABOUT OUR...*PAST* INSIDE CITY HALL.

YOU LOST ME.

JUST GOT BACK THE DENTAL RECORDS FROM THIS MORNING'S *BURNER.*

SHE WAS A 39-YEAR-OLD WOMAN NAMED ANDREA BREISS.

IS THAT SUPPOSED TO MEAN SOMETHING TO ME?

HER EX-HUSBAND WAS A GUY BY THE LAST NAME OF *SEVERTSON.*

THE BABY THEY HAD WHEN SHE WAS SIXTEEN WAS NAMED *CLEVELAND.*

CLEVELAND? THE...THE DEALER *THE GREAT MACHINE* BUSTED?

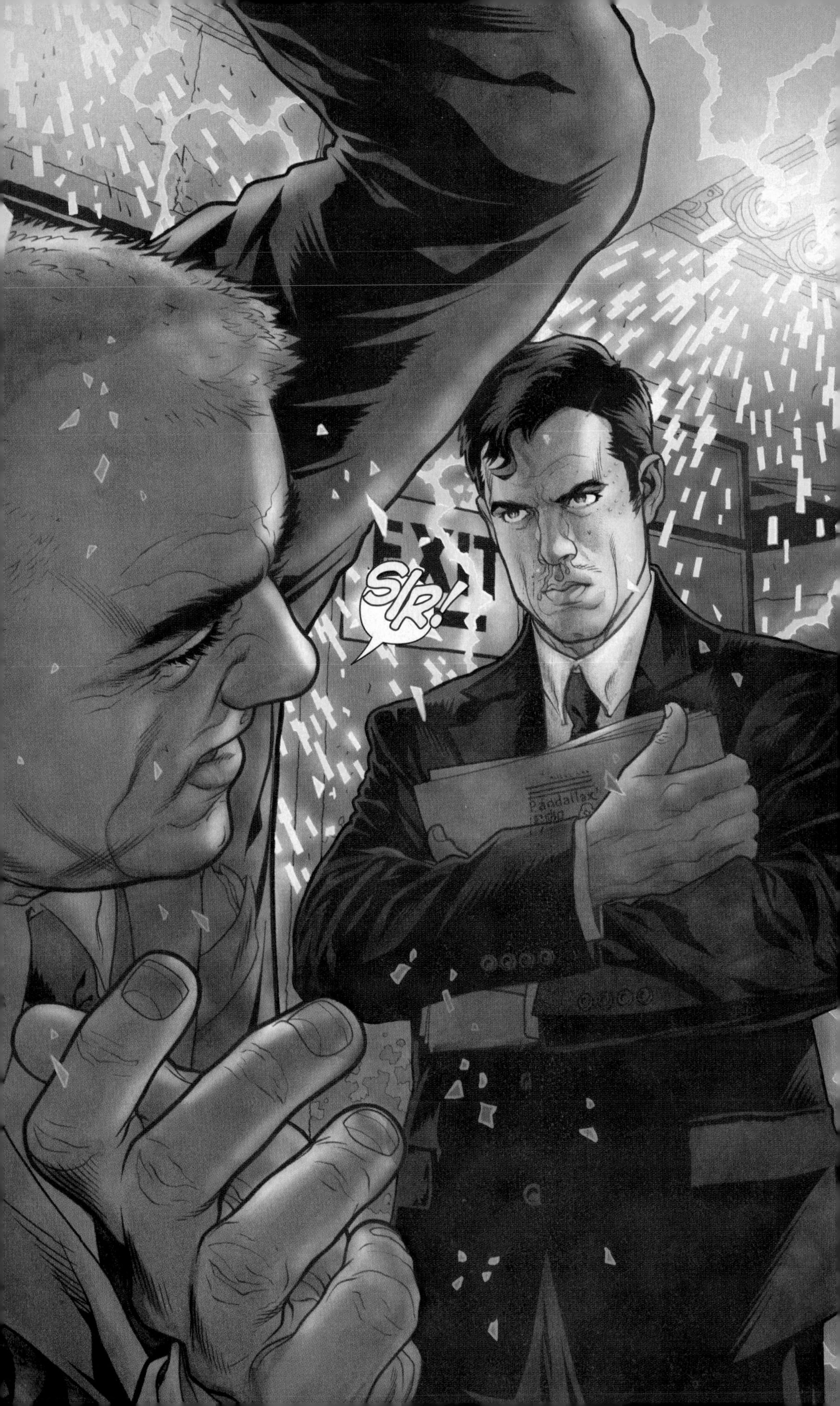
SIR!

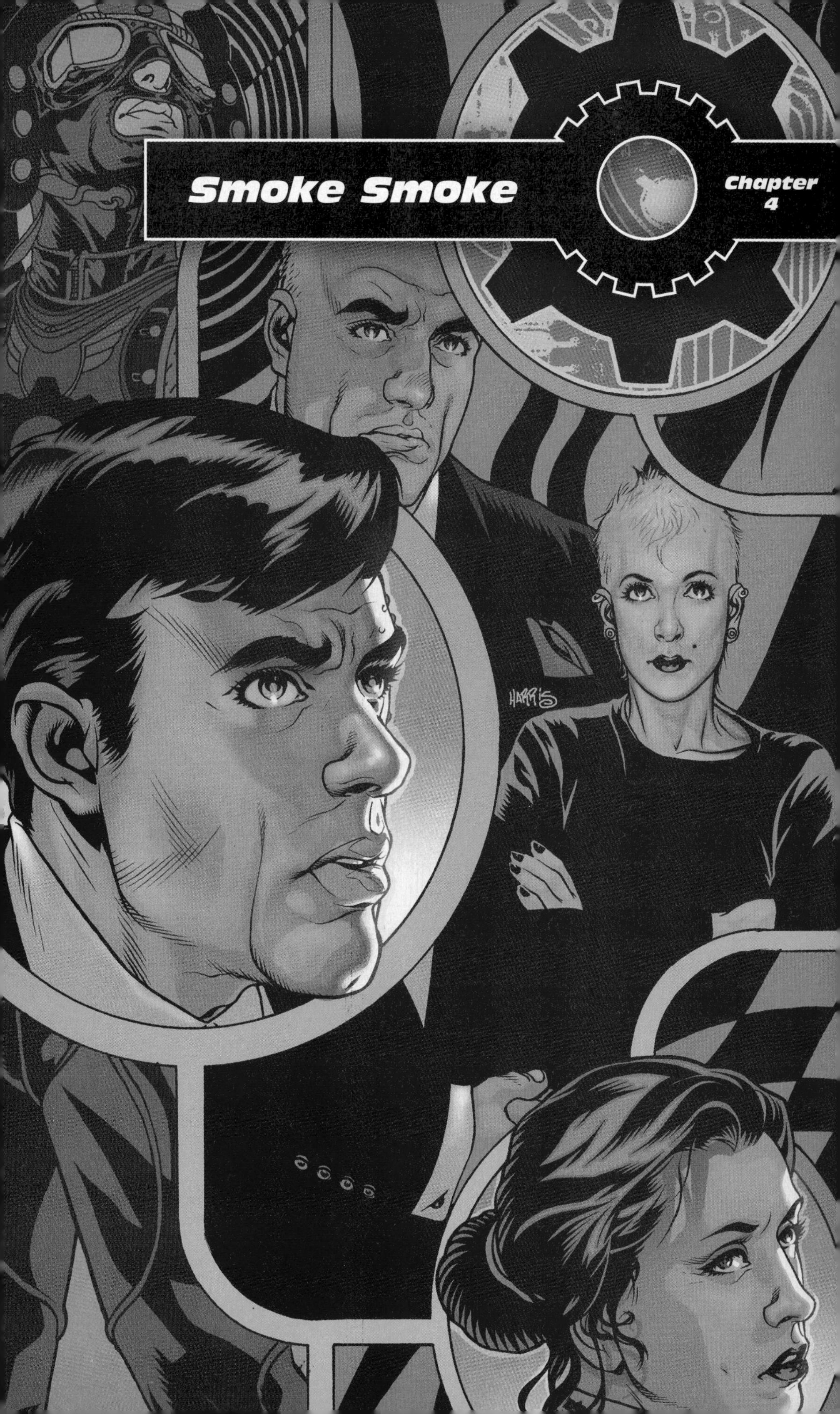
Smoke Smoke
Chapter 4
HARRIS

MONDAY, APRIL 2, 2001

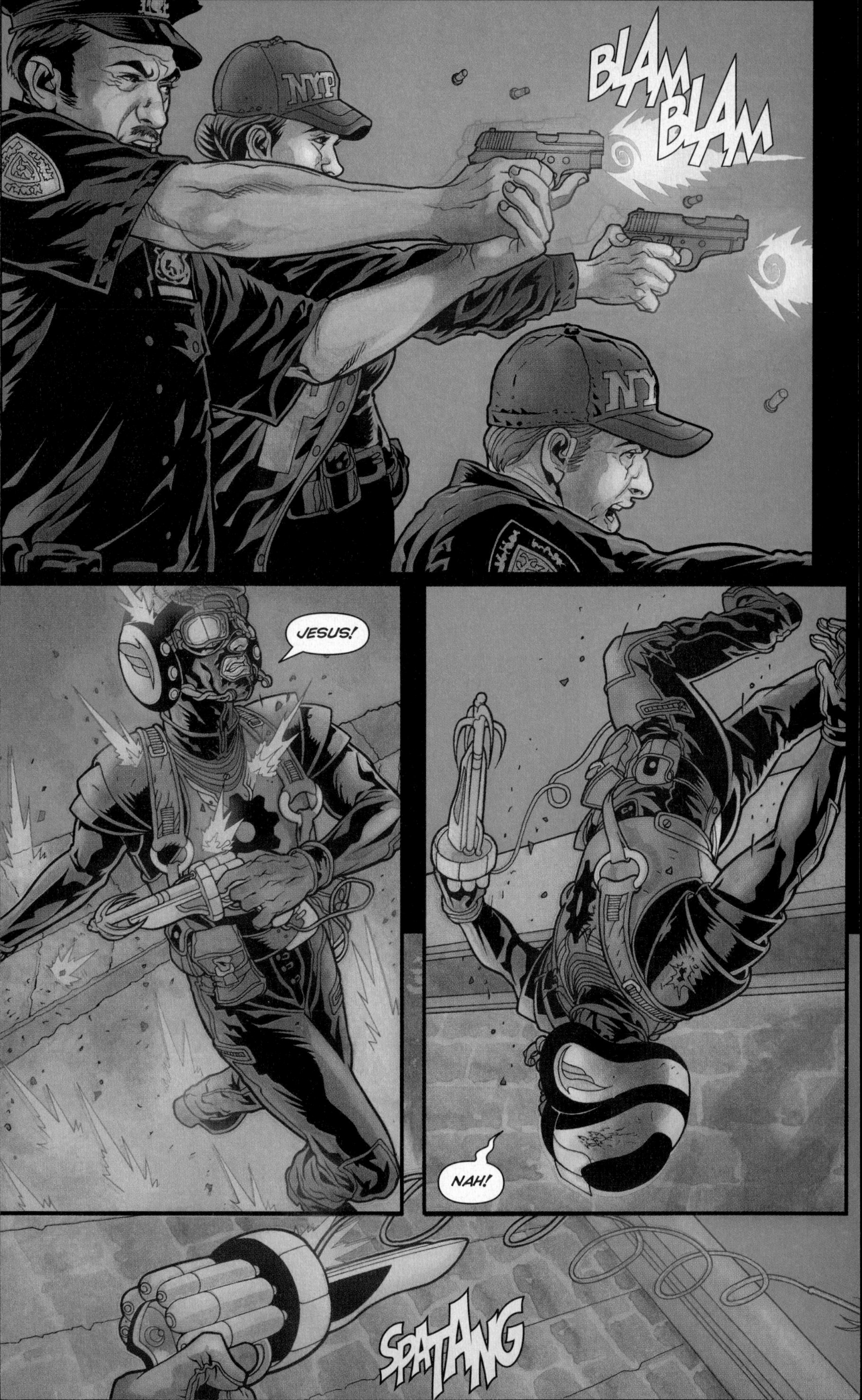
BLAM BLAM
JESUS!
NAH!
SPATANG

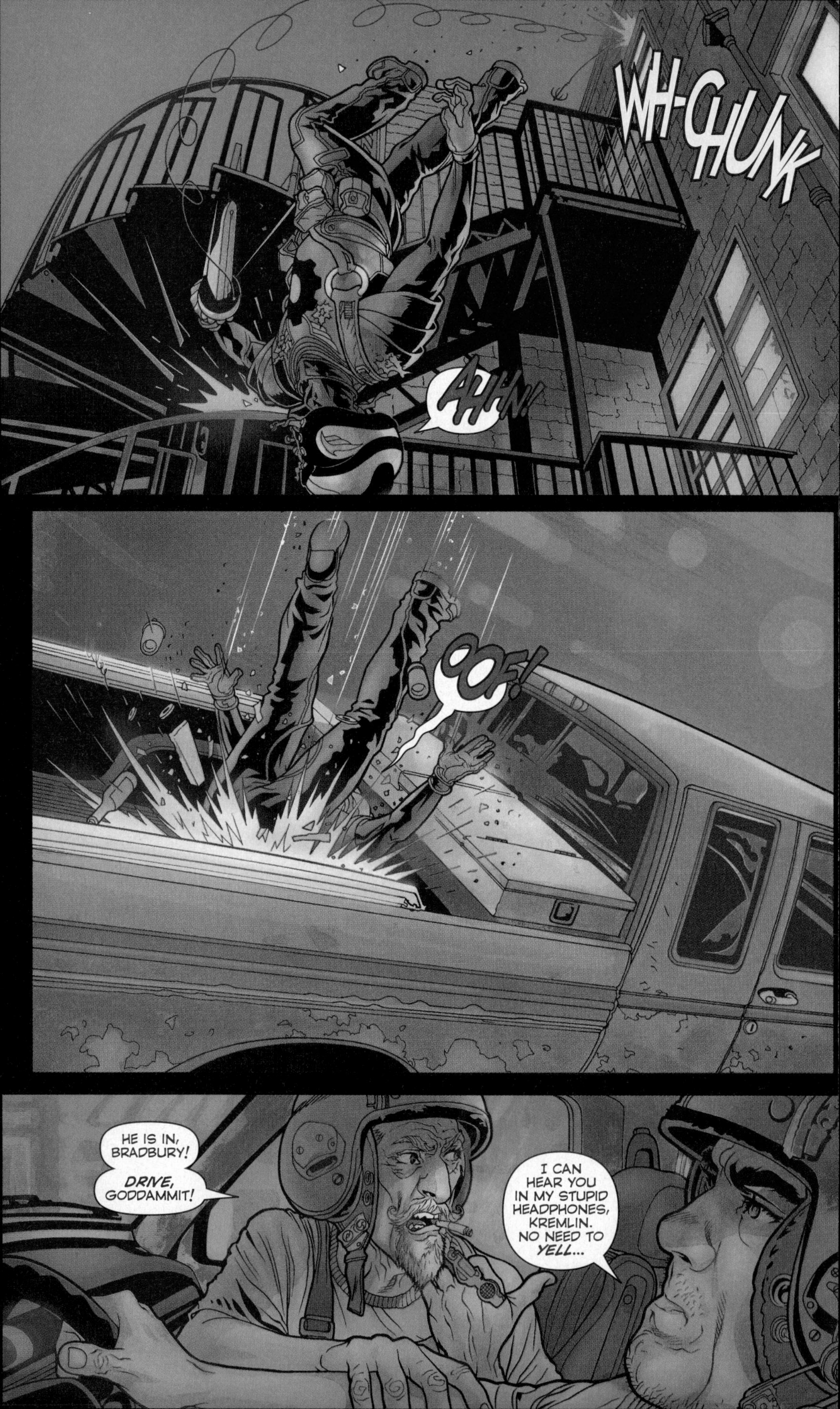
WH-CHUNK
AHHN!
OOF!
HE IS IN, BRADBURY!
DRIVE, GODDAMMIT!
I CAN HEAR YOU IN MY STUPID HEADPHONES, KREMLIN. NO NEED TO YELL...

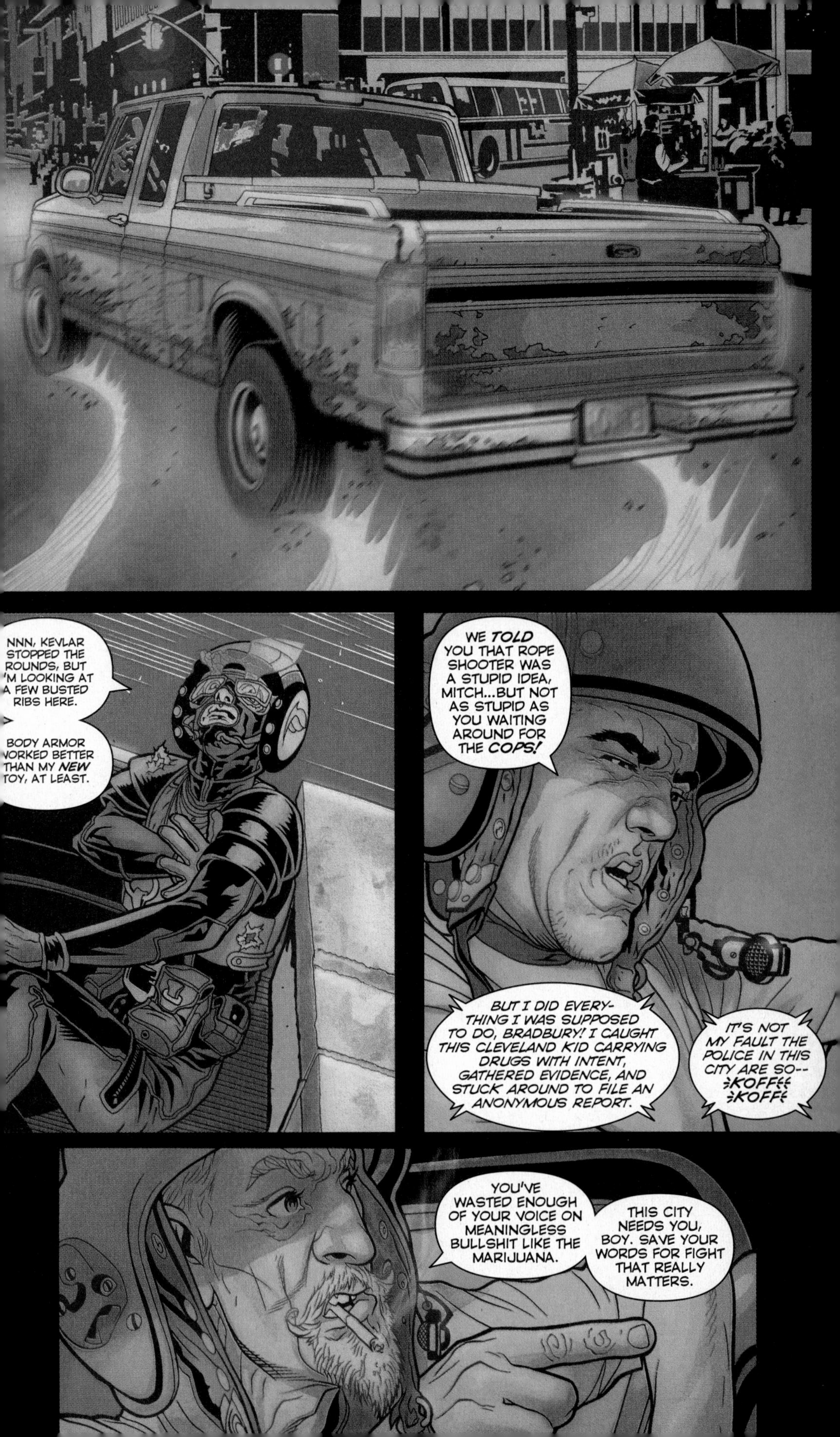
NNN, KEVLAR STOPPED THE ROUNDS, BUT I'M LOOKING AT A FEW BUSTED RIBS HERE.
BODY ARMOR WORKED BETTER THAN MY NEW TOY, AT LEAST.
WE TOLD YOU THAT ROPE SHOOTER WAS A STUPID IDEA, MITCH...BUT NOT AS STUPID AS YOU WAITING AROUND FOR THE COPS!
BUT I DID EVERYTHING I WAS SUPPOSED TO DO, BRADBURY! I CAUGHT THIS CLEVELAND KID CARRYING DRUGS WITH INTENT, GATHERED EVIDENCE, AND STUCK AROUND TO FILE AN ANONYMOUS REPORT.
IT'S NOT MY FAULT THE POLICE IN THIS CITY ARE SO-- KOFF KOFF
YOU'VE WASTED ENOUGH OF YOUR VOICE ON MEANINGLESS BULLSHIT LIKE THE MARIJUANA.
THIS CITY NEEDS YOU, BOY. SAVE YOUR WORDS FOR FIGHT THAT REALLY MATTERS.

TUESDAY, JULY 15, 2003

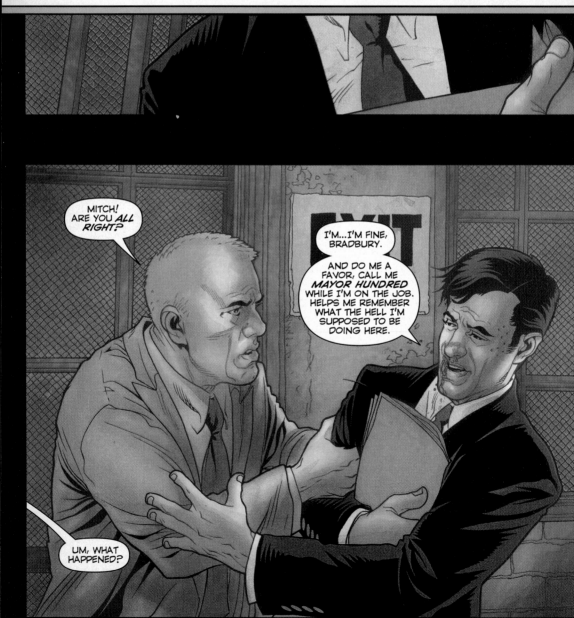

IS MY CAR OKAY?

GET THE FUCK OUT OF HERE, MAN!

A...A *TRANSFORMER* BLEW UP AND WE GOT LIVE WIRES ALL OVER!

WHO WAS THAT?

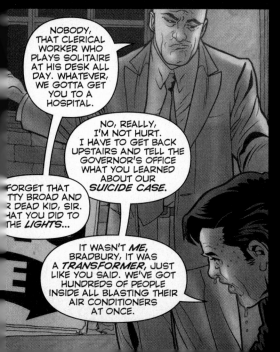

NOBODY, THAT CLERICAL WORKER WHO PLAYS SOLITAIRE AT HIS DESK ALL DAY. WHATEVER, WE GOTTA GET YOU TO A HOSPITAL.

NO, REALLY, I'M NOT HURT. I HAVE TO GET BACK UPSTAIRS AND TELL THE GOVERNOR'S OFFICE WHAT YOU LEARNED ABOUT OUR *SUICIDE CASE.*

FORGET THAT TTY BROAD AND R DEAD KID, SIR. HAT YOU DID TO THE *LIGHTS*...

IT WASN'T *ME*, BRADBURY, IT WAS A *TRANSFORMER*, JUST LIKE YOU SAID. WE'VE GOT HUNDREDS OF PEOPLE INSIDE ALL BLASTING THEIR AIR CONDITIONERS AT ONCE.

IT'S JUST STRESS ON THE SYSTEM.

I'VE BEEN LOOKING ALL OVER FOR YOU, SIR.

SORRY, JANUARY, I WAS DEALING WITH SOME POWER ISSUES.

WELL, I FOUND MORE STATS ON THE BENEFITS OF TREAT-MENT VERSUS INCARCERATION IN DRUG ARRESTS AND--

WHAT ABOUT COMMISSIONER ANGOTTI?

SHE'LL BE HERE IN FIFTEEN, TRAFFIC PENDING.

MR. MAYOR!

• • • •

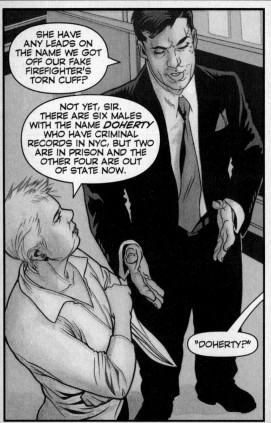

SHE HAVE ANY LEADS ON THE NAME WE GOT OFF OUR FAKE FIREFIGHTER'S TORN CUFF?

NOT YET, SIR. THERE ARE SIX MALES WITH THE NAME *DOHERTY* WHO HAVE CRIMINAL RECORDS IN NYC, BUT TWO ARE IN PRISON AND THE OTHER FOUR ARE OUT OF STATE NOW.

"DOHERTY?"

ISN'T HE A CHARACTER ON *THIRD WATCH?*

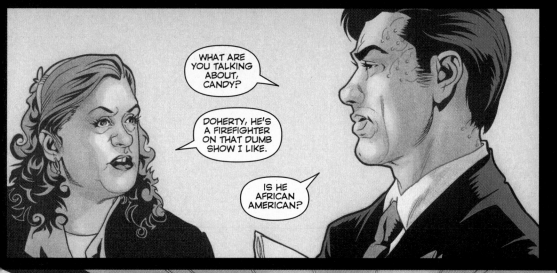

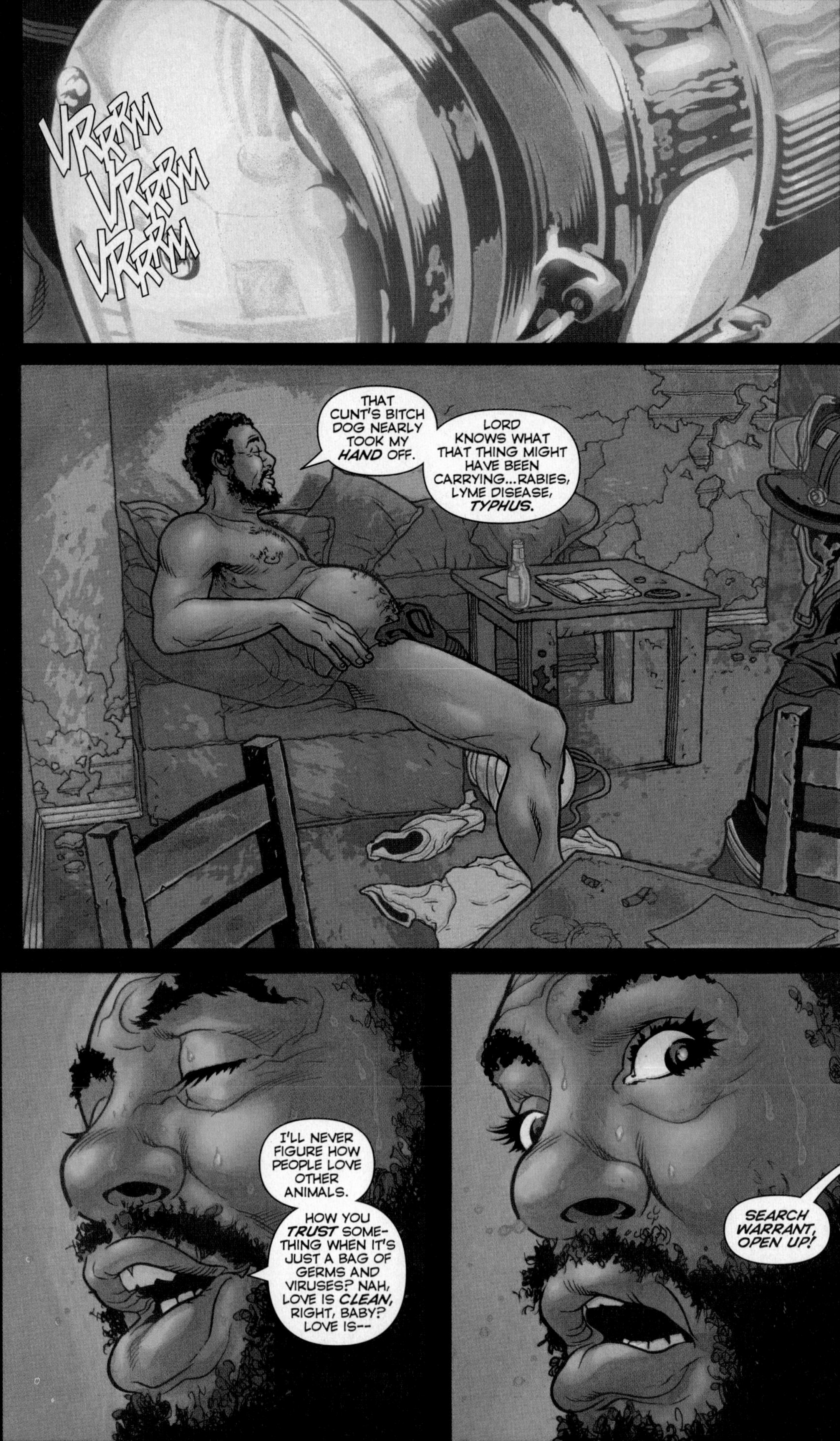

VRRRM VRRRM VRRRM
THAT CUNT'S BITCH DOG NEARLY TOOK MY HAND OFF.
LORD KNOWS WHAT THAT THING MIGHT HAVE BEEN CARRYING...RABIES, LYME DISEASE, TYPHUS.
I'LL NEVER FIGURE HOW PEOPLE LOVE OTHER ANIMALS.
HOW YOU TRUST SOME-THING WHEN IT'S JUST A BAG OF GERMS AND VIRUSES? NAH, LOVE IS CLEAN, RIGHT, BABY? LOVE IS--
SEARCH WARRANT, OPEN UP!

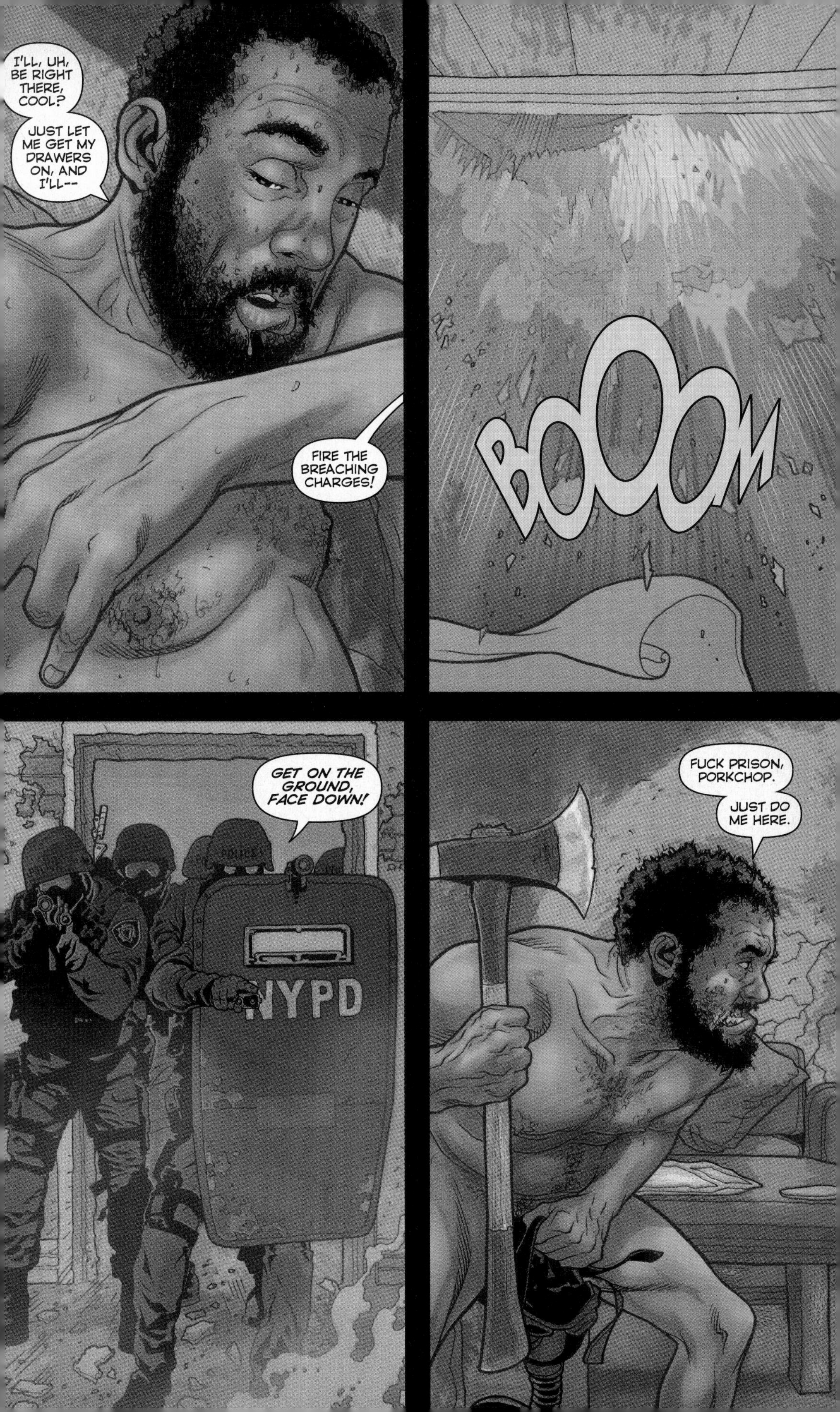
I'LL, UH, BE RIGHT THERE, COOL?
JUST LET ME GET MY DRAWERS ON, AND I'LL--
FIRE THE BREACHING CHARGES!
BOOOM
GET ON THE GROUND, FACE DOWN!
POLICE
NYPD
FUCK PRISON, PORKCHOP.
JUST DO ME HERE.

CLEAR!

≥GGNN≤

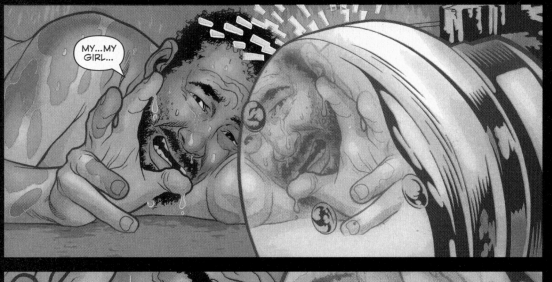

MY...MY GIRL...

NOT MY GIRL...

NO.

WE'RE NOT.

I'M NOT SUGGESTING, I'M *DECLARING*.

STARTING TODAY, WE'RE GOING TO LEAD THE CHARGE TO COMPLETELY OVERHAUL NEW YORK'S DRUG LAWS.

BUT, YOU WERE THE ONE WHO SAID THE ROCKEFELLER LAWS AMOUNTED TO INSTITUTIONALIZED RACISM, RIGHT? YOU SAID WE HAD TO REPEAL THEM AND--

THAT WAS BEFORE AN UNBALANCED WOMAN DECIDED TO PROTEST MANDATORY SENTENCES WITH A ZIPPO AND A GALLON OF *GASOLINE*.

WE START ADDRESSING HER GRIEVANCES IMMEDIATELY AFTER THAT STUNT, WE'LL HAVE EVERYONE FROM PETA TO PRO-LIFERS BARBECUING THEMSELVES OUT FRONT, TOO.

DAVE, SHE WAS A SICK WOMAN WHO DID SOMETHING PROFOUNDLY IDIOTIC, BUT IT DOESN'T CHANGE THE FACT THAT HER ANGER WAS *JUSTIFIED!*

DOESN'T MATTER. YOU'RE ABLE TO TACKLE THE MORE PROGRESSIVE SOCIAL ISSUES YOU WANT TO EXPLORE BECAUSE OF HOW CONSERVATIVE YOU'VE BEEN ON SECURITY.

IF YOU SUDDENLY LOOK LIKE YOU'RE GIVING IN TO THE DEMANDS OF "TERRORISTS," WE LOSE ON BOTH FRONTS.

SO INSTEAD OF GETTING BULLIED INTO TAKING THE *RIGHT* POSITION, WE GET INTIMIDATED INTO STICKING WITH THE *WRONG* ONE?

NO, WE CHANNEL OUR ENERGY BACK INTO *EDUCATION*, OPEN MORE HEAD START PROGRAMS TO KEEP KIDS FROM USING AND DEALING.

AND MUCH AS I HATE TO SAY IT, WE'RE GOING TO HAVE TO START COOPERATING WITH TRIP IN THE *GOVERNOR'S OFFICE* IF WE'RE EVER GOING TO--

UHHHHH...

SIR!

IT'S NOTHING. JUST...JUST A DIZZY SPELL.

YOU HAVE *GOT* TO SLOW DOWN.

DEDICATION TO THE OFFICE IS WELL AND FINE, BUT YOU WOULDN'T BE THE FIRST MAN TO DROP DEAD OF A HEART ATTACK AT *THIRTY-FIVE.*

THAT'S MORE YEARS THAN SOME PEOPLE GET.

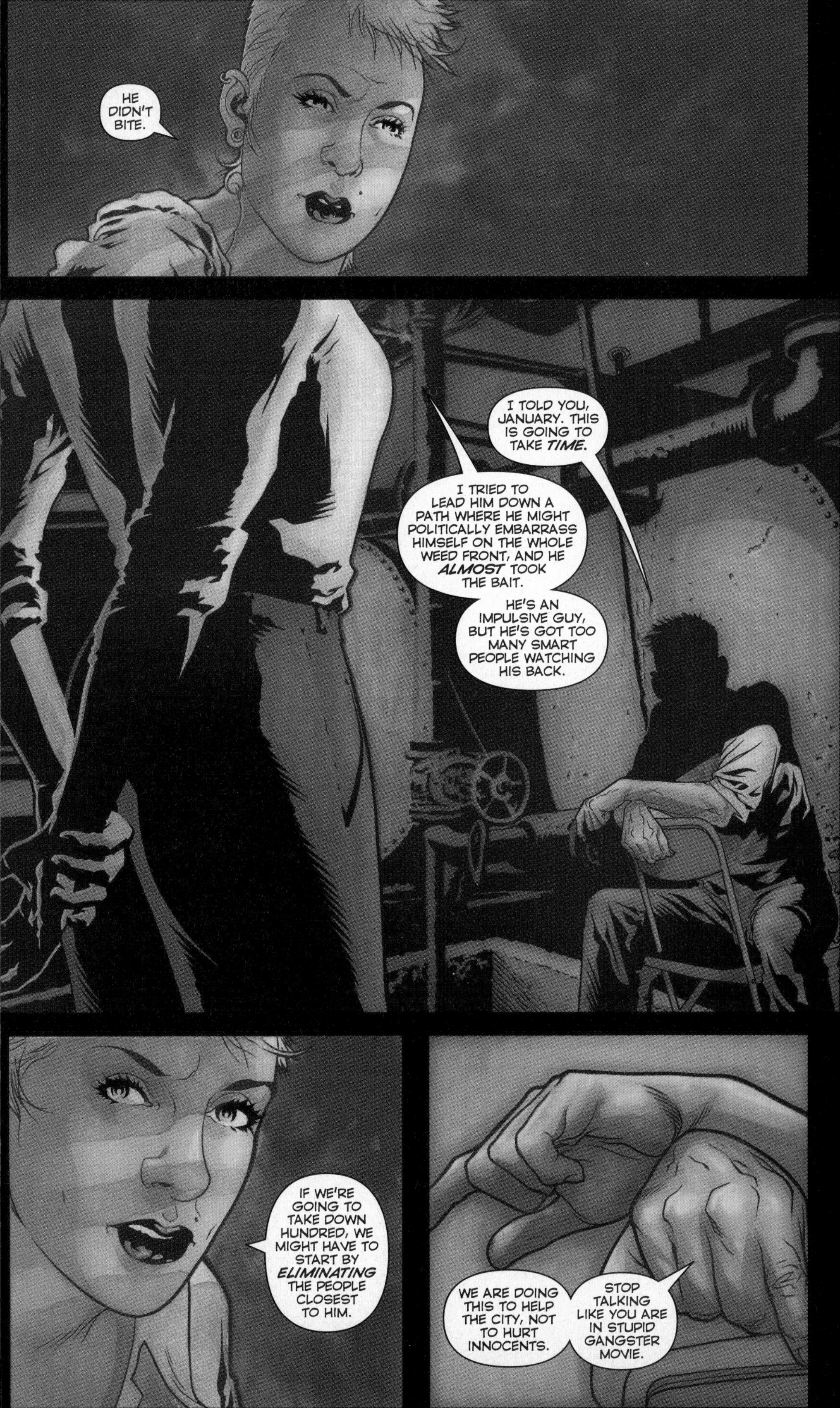
HE DIDN'T BITE.
I TOLD YOU, JANUARY. THIS IS GOING TO TAKE *TIME*.
I TRIED TO LEAD HIM DOWN A PATH WHERE HE MIGHT POLITICALLY EMBARRASS HIMSELF ON THE WHOLE WEED FRONT, AND HE *ALMOST* TOOK THE BAIT.
HE'S AN IMPULSIVE GUY, BUT HE'S GOT TOO MANY SMART PEOPLE WATCHING HIS BACK.
IF WE'RE GOING TO TAKE DOWN HUNDRED, WE MIGHT HAVE TO START BY *ELIMINATING* THE PEOPLE CLOSEST TO HIM.
STOP TALKING LIKE YOU ARE IN STUPID GANGSTER MOVIE.
WE ARE DOING THIS TO HELP THE CITY, NOT TO HURT INNOCENTS.

LANDMARKS OF NEW YORK

GRACIE MANSION

BUILT ABOUT 1799 ON THE SITE OF A
REVOLUTIONARY FORT AS THE COUNTRY
HOUSE OF ARCHIBALD GRACIE, SCOTTISH
MERCHANT. THIS COLONIAL STRUCTURE WAS

SECURITY SYSTEM REACTIVATED BY HUNDRED.

TIVO HAS RECORDED "IN THE PAPERS" ON NY1. TIVO HAS RECORDED "NBC NIGHTLY NEWS" ON NBC. TIVO HAS--

ANSWERING MACHINE FLASHES TWELVE MESSAGES. ANSWERING MACHINE FLASHES TWELVE MESSAGES.

HUNDRED TURNS HALLWAY LIGHT TO ON.

CLIMATE CONTROL SET TO SEVENTY-NINE DEGREES. FAN ON.

11:56 P.M. AND FIFTEEN SECONDS. 11:56 P.M. AND SIXTEEN SECONDS.

DESK LAMP IS OFF.

11:56 P.M. AND TWENTY SECONDS. 11:56 P.M. AND TWENTY-ONE SECONDS.

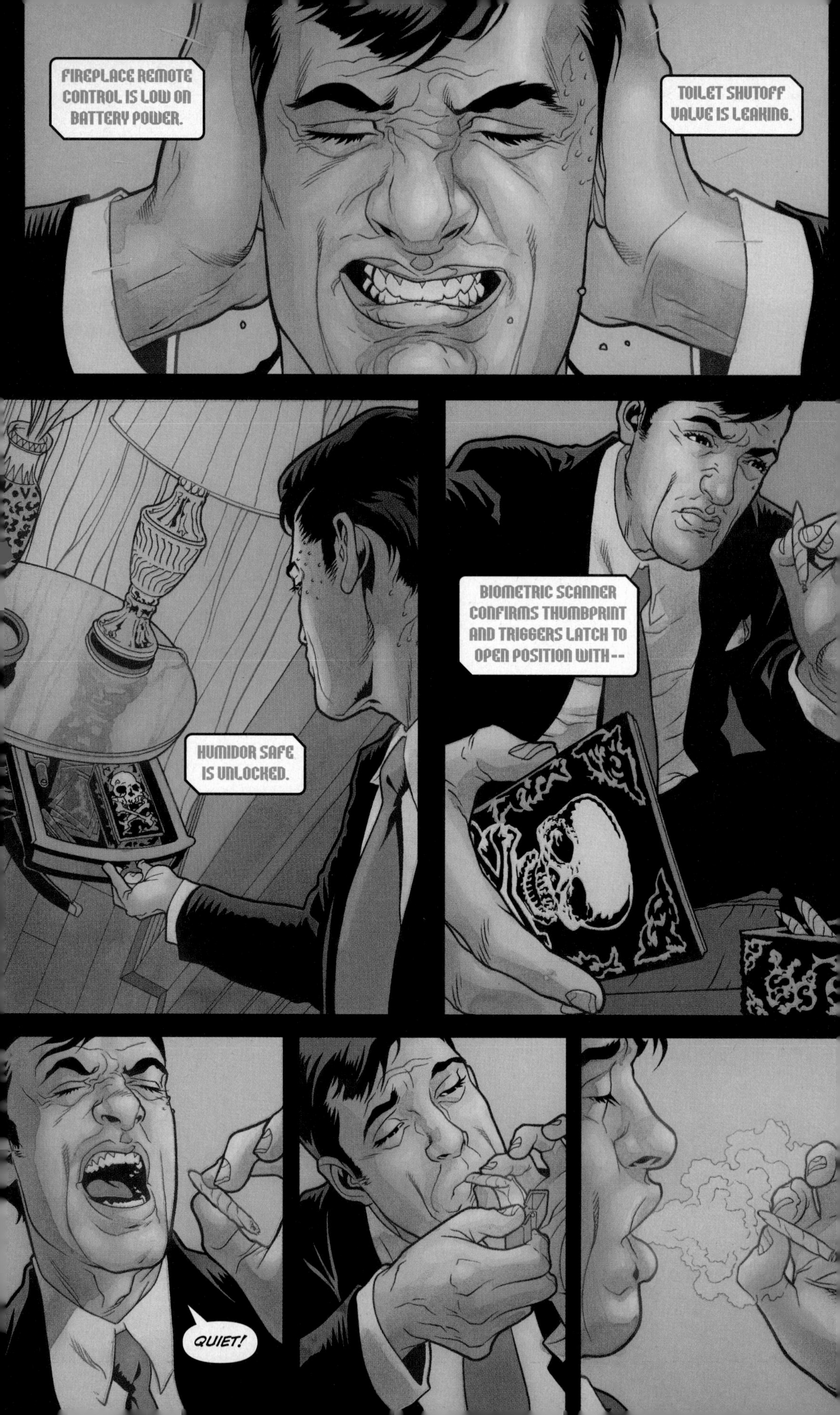
FIREPLACE REMOTE CONTROL IS LOW ON BATTERY POWER.
TOILET SHUTOFF VALVE IS LEAKING.
HUMIDOR SAFE IS UNLOCKED.
BIOMETRIC SCANNER CONFIRMS THUMBPRINT AND TRIGGERS LATCH TO OPEN POSITION WITH--
QUIET!

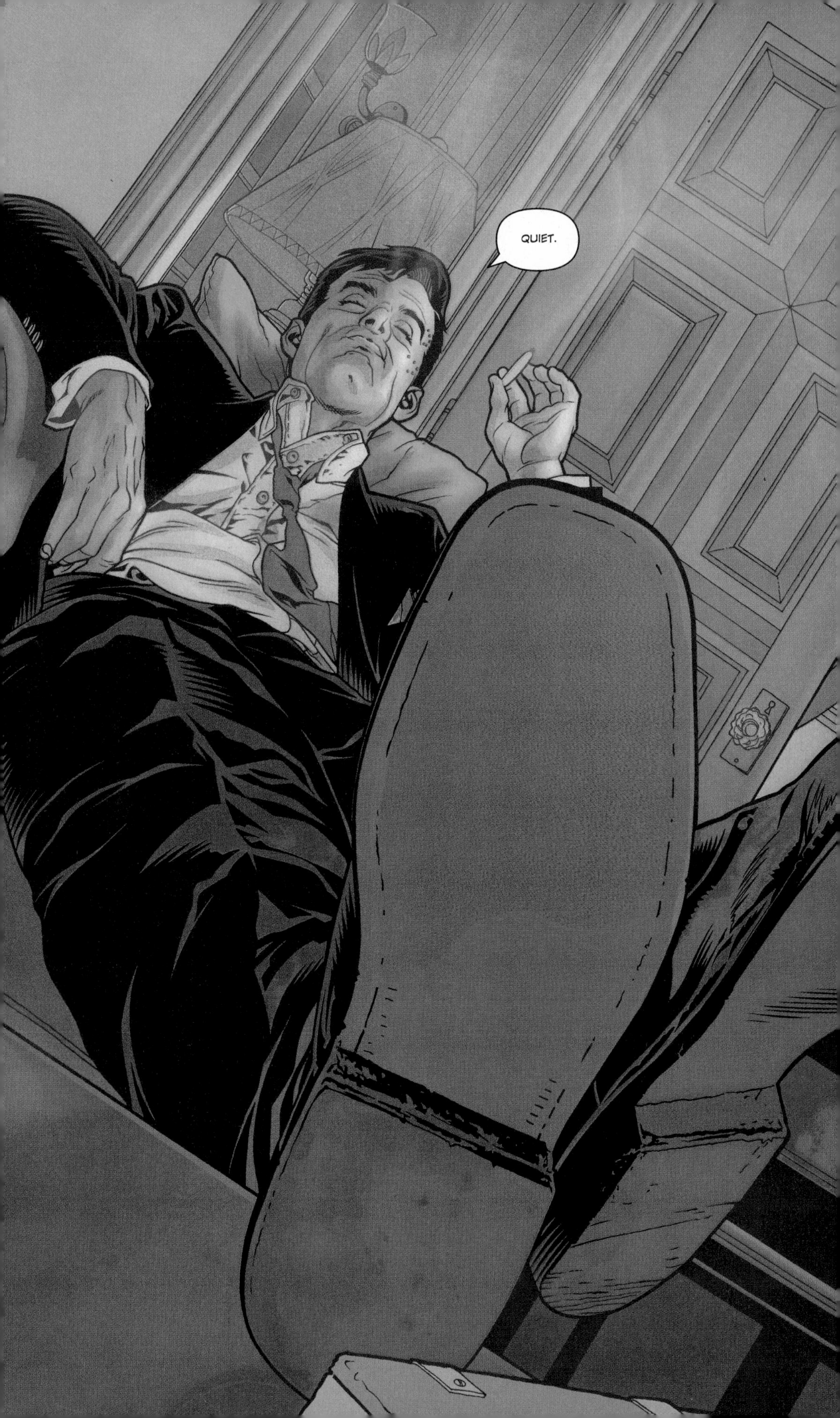
QUIET.

Chapter 5

Standalone

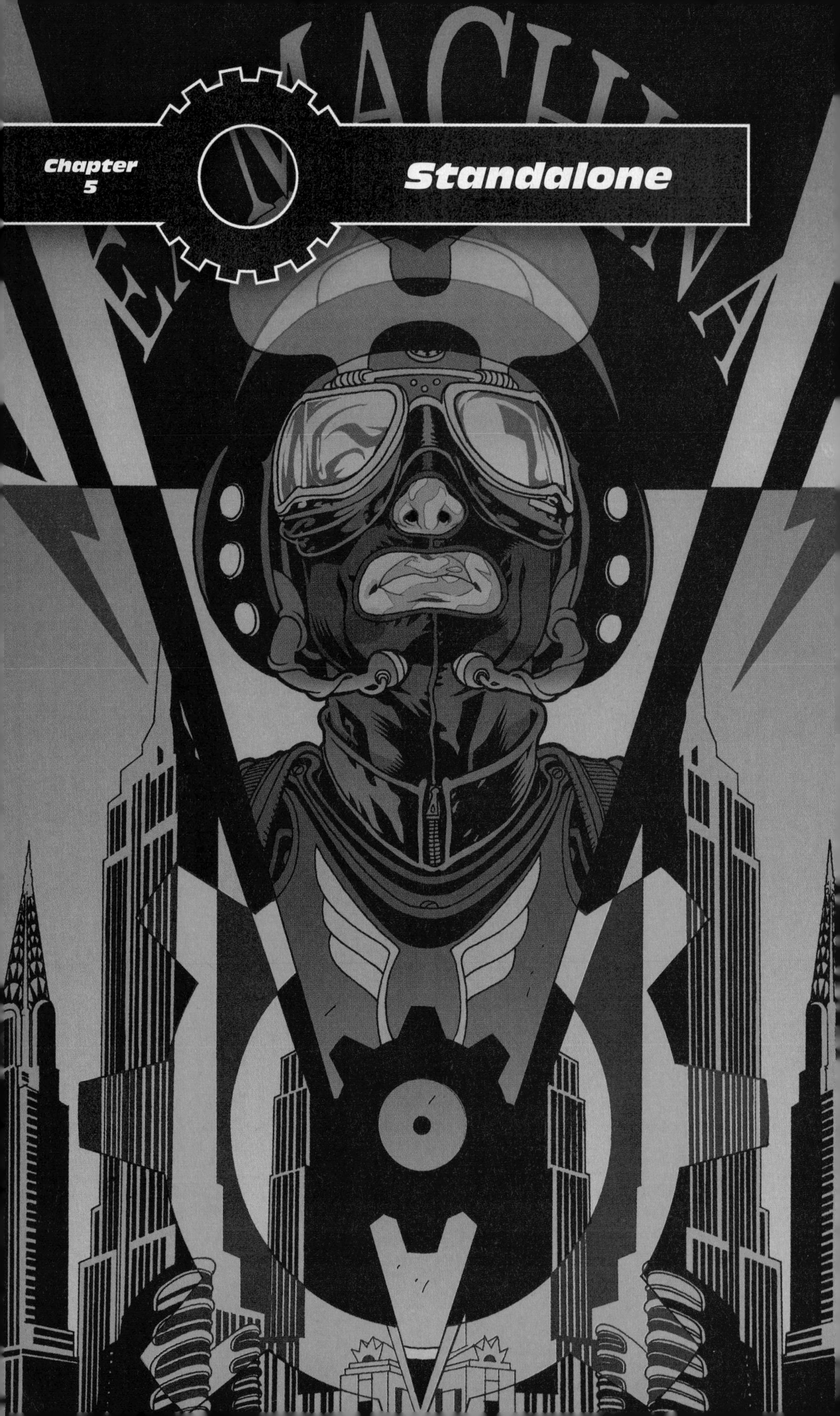

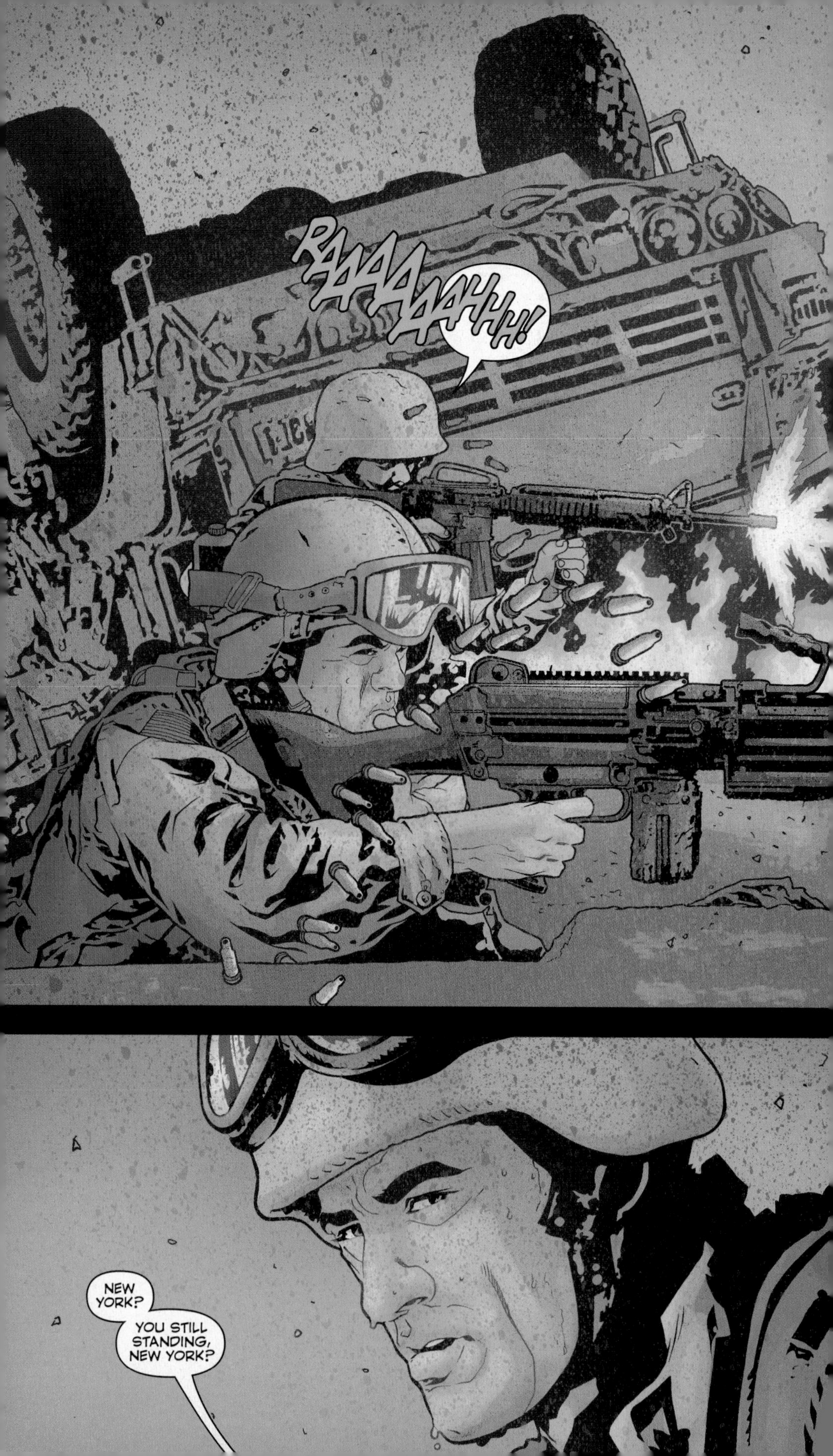
RAAAAAAHHH!
NEW YORK?
YOU STILL STANDING, NEW YORK?

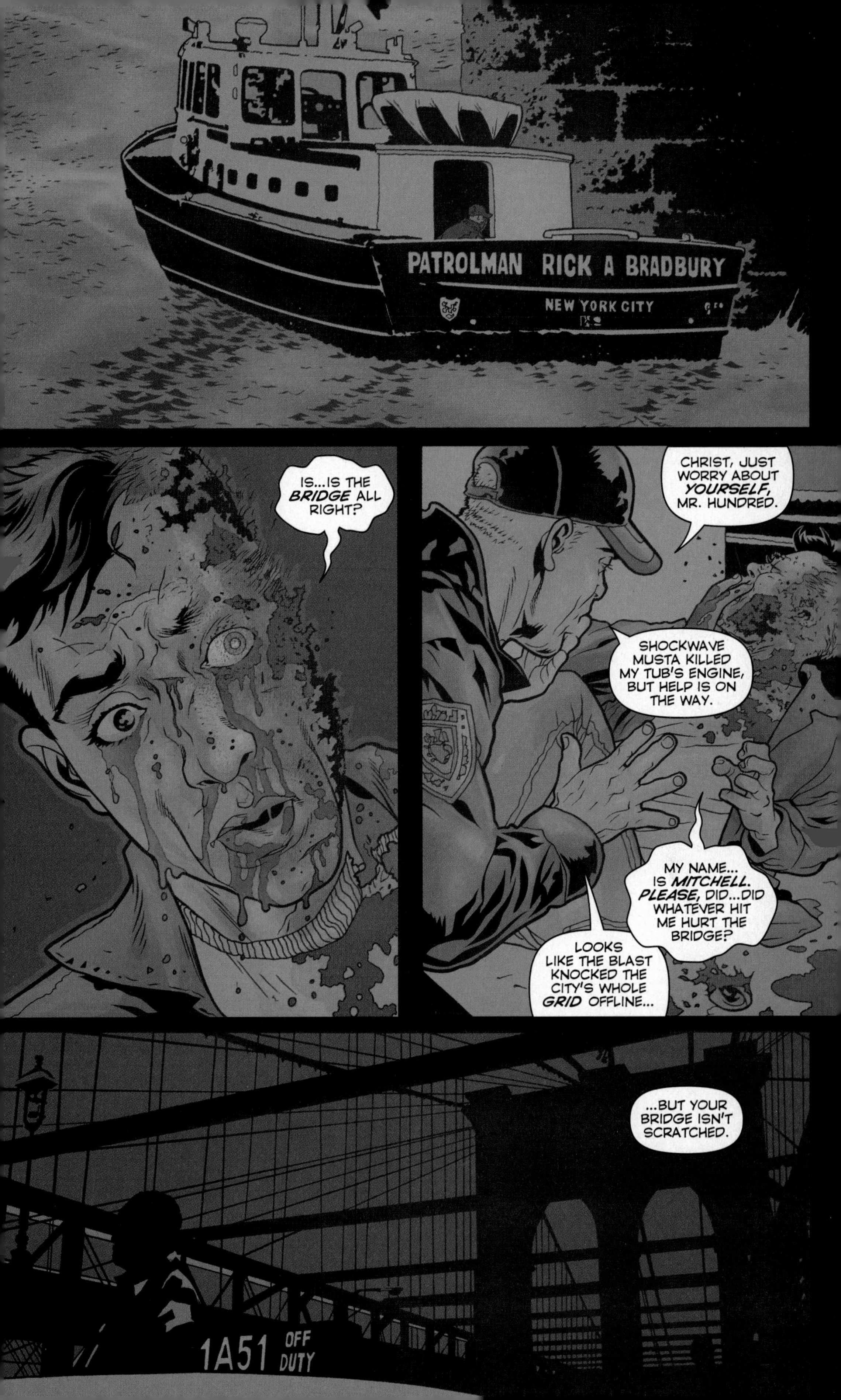
PATROLMAN RICK A BRADBURY
NEW YORK CITY
IS...IS THE BRIDGE ALL RIGHT?
CHRIST, JUST WORRY ABOUT YOURSELF, MR. HUNDRED.
SHOCKWAVE MUSTA KILLED MY TUB'S ENGINE, BUT HELP IS ON THE WAY.
MY NAME... IS MITCHELL. PLEASE, DID...DID WHATEVER HIT ME HURT THE BRIDGE?
LOOKS LIKE THE BLAST KNOCKED THE CITY'S WHOLE GRID OFFLINE...
...BUT YOUR BRIDGE ISN'T SCRATCHED.
1A51 OFF DUTY

ALL TRAFFIC CAMERAS ON THIS BLOCK, KINDLY DELETE ANY FOOTAGE OF MY PARTNERS. WOULD YOU?

I'M GONNA TRY TO GET PHERSON TO THE *DEPRIVATION TANK* I BUILT BEFORE HIS *BATS* CATCH UP WITH ME!

KREM, TRACK ME ON G.P.S. AND KEEP ME APPRISED OF MY FUEL SITCH!

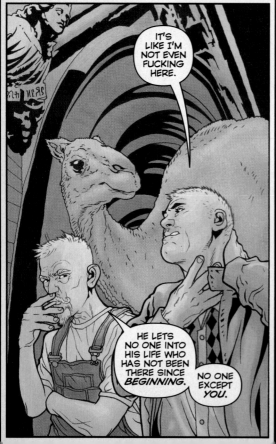

IT'S LIKE I'M NOT EVEN FUCKING HERE.

HE LETS NO ONE INTO HIS LIFE WHO HAS NOT BEEN THERE SINCE *BEGINNING*.

NO ONE EXCEPT *YOU*.

YEAH? WHY? YOU THINK HE SEES A BIT OF HIMSELF IN ME?

NO, DUMMY, IN YOU HE SEES *CHAUFFEUR*.

HE MIGHT BE ABLE TO HAVE CONVERSATIONS WITH CARS, BUT MITCHELL STILL DRIVES FOR *SHIT*.

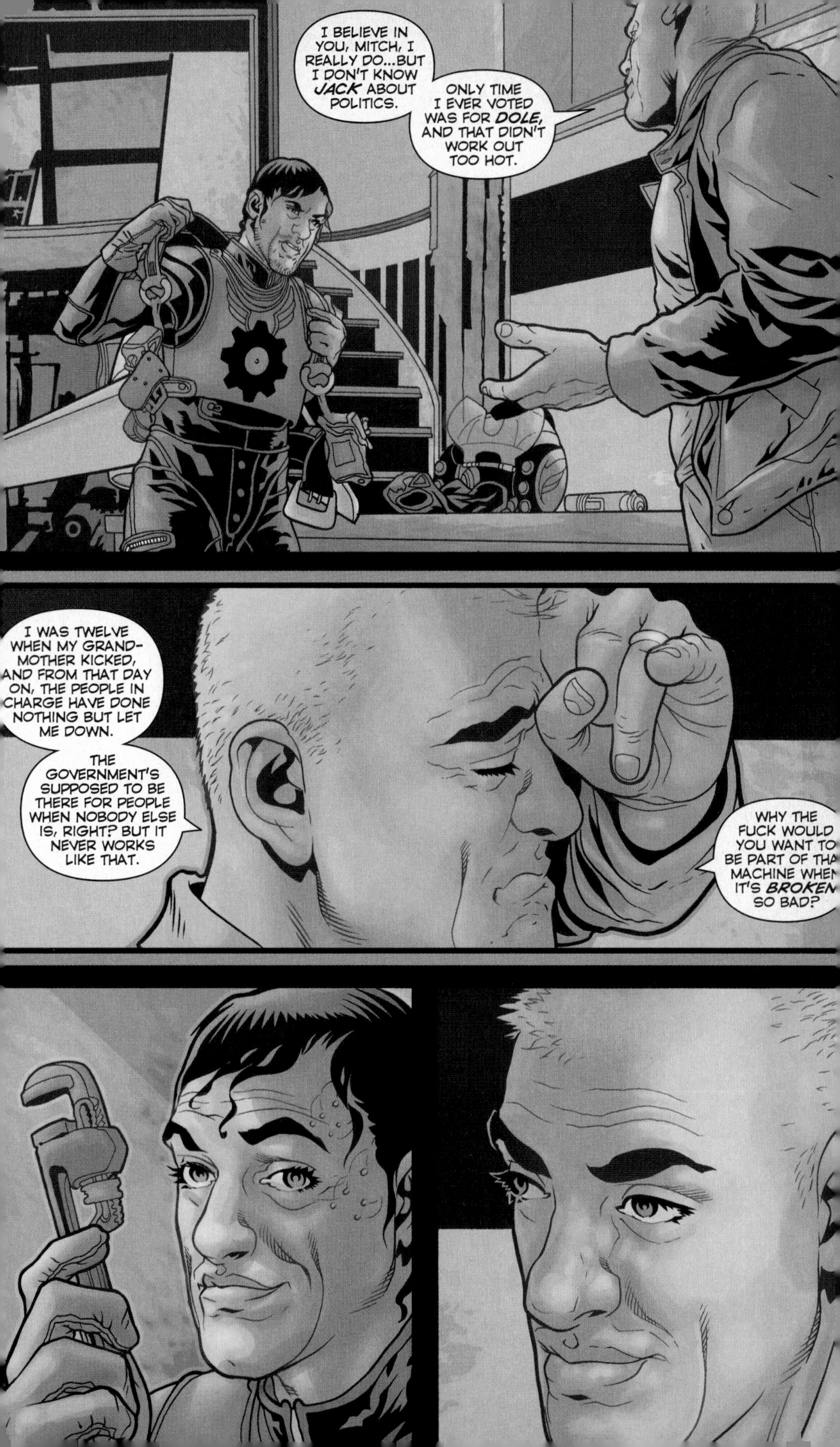
I BELIEVE IN YOU, MITCH, I REALLY DO...BUT I DON'T KNOW *JACK* ABOUT POLITICS.
ONLY TIME I EVER VOTED WAS FOR *DOLE,* AND THAT DIDN'T WORK OUT TOO HOT.
I WAS TWELVE WHEN MY GRAND-MOTHER KICKED, AND FROM THAT DAY ON, THE PEOPLE IN CHARGE HAVE DONE NOTHING BUT LET ME DOWN.
THE GOVERNMENT'S SUPPOSED TO BE THERE FOR PEOPLE WHEN NOBODY ELSE IS, RIGHT? BUT IT NEVER WORKS LIKE THAT.
WHY THE FUCK WOULD YOU WANT TO BE PART OF THA MACHINE WHEN IT'S *BROKEN* SO BAD?

DON'T DO IT, MAN.

SORRY, YOUR VOICE IS NOT QUITE AS PERSUASIVE AS YOUR *MASTER'S*.

WHICH IS WHY HE CALLED HIS BUDDIES IN THE CIA, FBI, NSA, NYPD, AND MORE ACRONYMS THAN A BOWL OF FUCKING *ALPHABET SOUP*...

...AND HAD A DOZEN OF THEIR BEST SNIPERS HELP ME SET UP THIS LITTLE *TRAP*.

HE'S NOT MY *MASTER*, HE'S MY *FRIEND*...WHICH IS WHY HE WATCHES *MY* SIX WHILE I WATCH HIS.

HE'S THE ONE WHO FIRST SPOTTED YOU TRAILING ME A WEEK AGO, ON BROADWAY AND 45TH. AND TWO DAYS AGO AT THE CARNEGIE HALL ROPE-LINE. AND OUTSIDE MY APARTMENT YESTERDAY.

...

BULLSHIT.

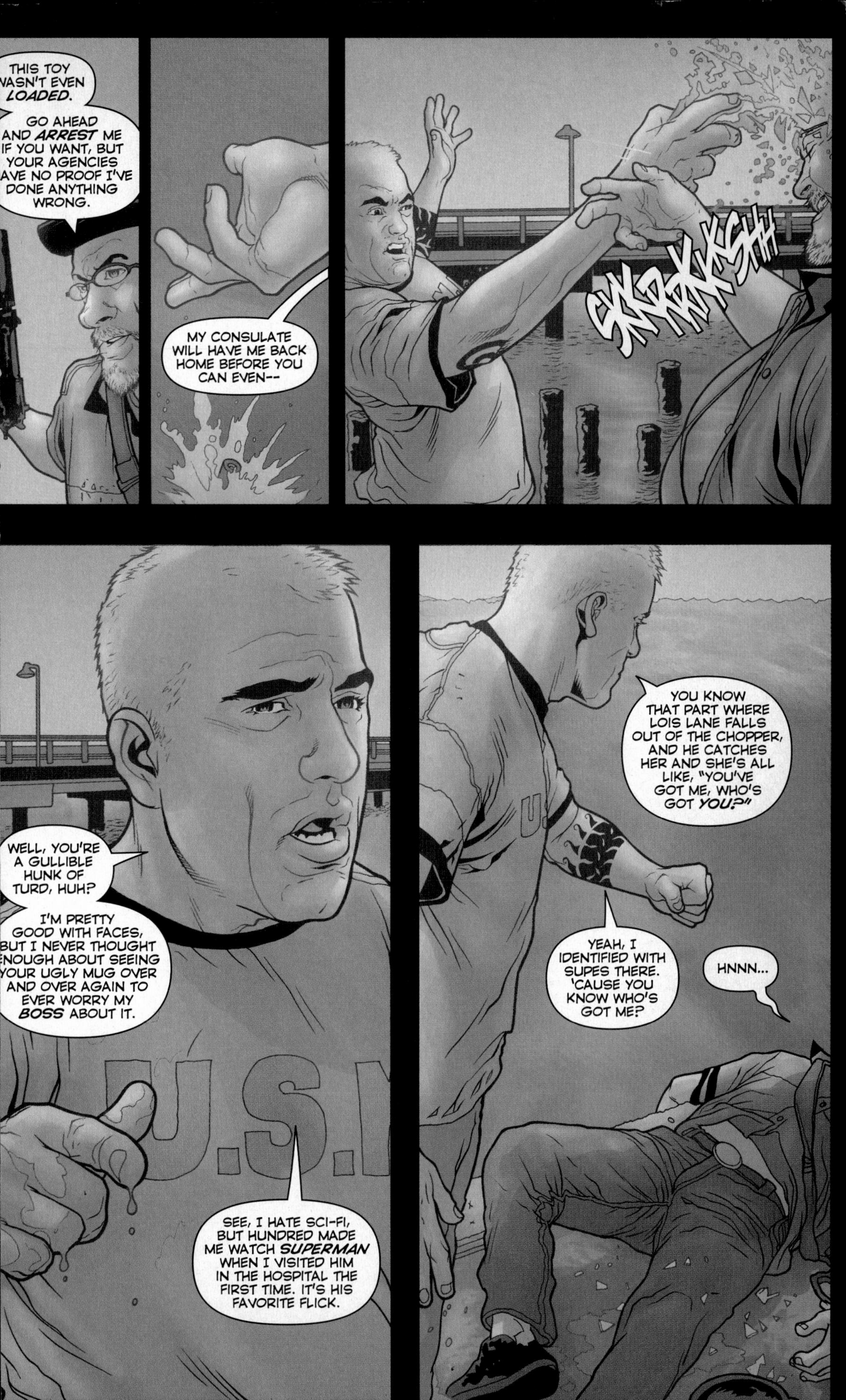

THIS TOY WASN'T EVEN *LOADED*.
GO AHEAD AND *ARREST* ME IF YOU WANT, BUT YOUR AGENCIES HAVE NO PROOF I'VE DONE ANYTHING WRONG.
MY CONSULATE WILL HAVE ME BACK HOME BEFORE YOU CAN EVEN--
SKRAKKSH
WELL, YOU'RE A GULLIBLE HUNK OF TURD, HUH?
I'M PRETTY GOOD WITH FACES, BUT I NEVER THOUGHT ENOUGH ABOUT SEEING YOUR UGLY MUG OVER AND OVER AGAIN TO EVER WORRY MY *BOSS* ABOUT IT.
SEE, I HATE SCI-FI, BUT HUNDRED MADE ME WATCH *SUPERMAN* WHEN I VISITED HIM IN THE HOSPITAL THE FIRST TIME. IT'S HIS FAVORITE FLICK.
YOU KNOW THAT PART WHERE LOIS LANE FALLS OUT OF THE CHOPPER, AND HE CATCHES HER AND SHE'S ALL LIKE, "YOU'VE GOT ME, WHO'S GOT *YOU?*"
YEAH, I IDENTIFIED WITH SUPES THERE. 'CAUSE YOU KNOW WHO'S GOT ME?
HNNN...

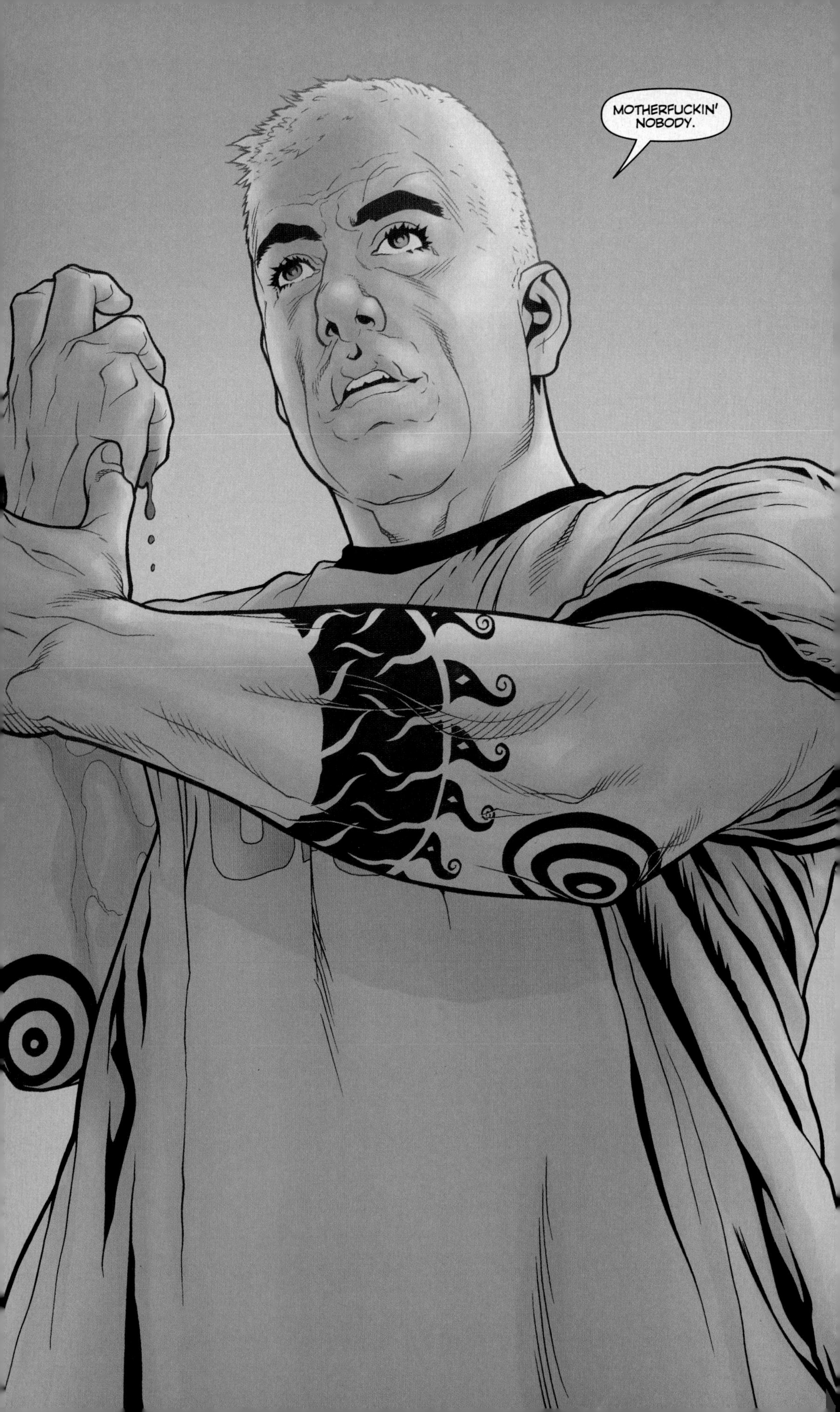
MOTHERFUCKIN' NOBODY.

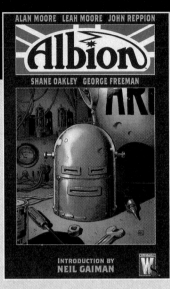
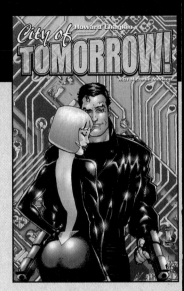